# STORYMAKING IN ELEMENTARY AND MIDDLE SCHOOL CLASSROOMS

## Constructing and Interpreting Narrative Texts

# STORYMAKING IN ELEMENTARY AND MIDDLE SCHOOL CLASSROOMS

## Constructing and Interpreting Narrative Texts

Joanne M. Golden
*University of Delaware*

**IEA** LAWRENCE ERLBAUM ASSOCIATES, PUBLISHERS
2000  Mahwah, New Jersey                    London

Lawrence Erlbaum Associates, Inc., Publishers
10 Industrial Avenue
Mahwah, New Jersey 07430-2262

Cover design by Kathryn Houghtaling Lacey

Library of Congress Cataloging-in-Publication Data

Golden, Joanne Marie, 1949–
    Storymaking in elementary and middle school classrooms :
constructing and interpreting narrative texts / Joanne M. Golden.
        p.  cm.
    Includes bibliographical references and index.
    ISBN 0-8058-3287-4 (pbk. : alk. paper)
    1. Storytelling. 2. Discourse analysis, Narrative. 3. Reading (Elementary). 4. Reading (Middle school). I. Title.
LB1042.G54 2000
372.67'7—dc21                                                                    99-37883
                                                                                            CIP

Books published by Lawrence Erlbaum Associates are printed on acid-free paper, and their bindings are chosen for strength and durability

Printed in the United States of America
10  9  8  7  6  5  4  3  2  1

*To my sister, Donna Canan,*
*for her caring, support, and dedication*

# Contents

## I: SOCIAL SEMIOTICS AND CLASSROOM TEXTS

## II: STORYMAKING IN CLASSROOMS

## III: ISSUES, DIRECTIONS, AND TEXTUAL PRACTICES

# Preface

## AN APPROACH TO THIS BOOK

One basic aim of this text is to examine factors related to authors' texts and readers' roles in transforming these texts into stories. A second, and more central, goal is to consider how the social discourse in which the text is embedded shapes the story that unfolds. These analyses provide the basis for exploring issues related to the development of textual capabilities in classroom settings. Such an exploration requires a close examination of text and discourse and an analysis of their dialogic relations during classroom events. The systems for examining and analyzing the text, reader, and discourse inevitably influence what is seen because interpretations of events are constructed through the lenses of the analytical systems that are applied.

In this volume, the analytical approaches are drawn from different discipline areas, including social semiotics, narrative theory, cognitive psychology, and research on teaching. This approach reflects the view that understanding classroom events is facilitated by multiple-perspective analyses (Green & Harker, 1987).

The data for these analyses are drawn from the author's current and previous studies of text–student–teacher interactions in a variety of classrooms at different grade levels. For the purposes of this volume, data from previous studies are (re)examined or new data are analyzed to explore the interaction between the author's text and the reader's processes and the nature and influence of the student(s)–teacher exchange on storymaking processes. Segments from authors' texts and classroom events are used to illustrate theoretical points regarding social and academic expectations for storymaking in particular contexts. The intent is not to generalize about storymaking processes in classroom contexts. These data therefore function as heuristic tools for exploring key dimensions of meaning making processes.

In reading this volume, you are engaged in a semiotic process that involves transforming authors' and participants' words derived from the classroom data and my text, which frames these data. To identify the multiple voices in the volume, three types of print are used: my text is in regular print; *italics* are used for teachers' and students' voices; and **Swiss** for the narrative author's words. My interpretations reflect one lens for viewing storymaking that will coincide, to some extent, with interpretations of others who share a similar theoretical framework and use comparable systems of interpretive analysis. Those who use other frameworks and ways of looking can challenge, modify, extend, or confirm observations against their own educational and research experiences. Whatever the vantage point, no one interpreter can assume the position of an authority whose reading supersedes all other readings because of the indeterminacy of meaning in texts and text events. The readers of this volume, therefore, are invited to assume the role of an active participant who "reads" and transforms authors' texts into stories and storymaking events in classrooms.

## ORGANIZATION OF THE VOLUME

Part I, Social Semiotics and Classroom Texts, includes chapters 1 and 2. In chapter 1, a social semiotic perspective on storymaking in classrooms is developed. Classrooms are discussed as unique semiotic systems in which authors' texts are embedded in social discourse. Chapter 2 focuses on the signals for constructing narrative elements in the authors' texts. Particular emphasis is placed on the elements of narrator, time, and character.

Part II, Storymaking in Classrooms, includes chapters 3 through 6. In chapter 3, storymaking processes in classroom events function as potential signs open to analysis. Story texts are examined in the context of the social discourse occurring between teacher and student, stressing how teachers mediate the author's text for the students. Whereas chapter 3 centers on the teacher's role as mediator during the unfolding of the text (e.g., a storybook reading event), chapter 4 explores how participants construct the reactive texts after the reading process (e.g., the postreading discussions). Along these lines, chapter 5 views various types of students' reactive texts (e.g., journal responses). In chapter 6, storymaking events in one teacher's classroom illustrate intertextual relations between events and the building of a storymaking community. Chapters 3 through 6 then provide frameworks for analyzing the process of constructing and interpreting text, the social discourse in which the text is embedded, and the dialogic relationship between the two.

Part III, Issues, Directions, and Textual Practices, includes chapters 7 and 8. In chapter 7, issues and questions related to developing storymaking capabilities in classroom settings are addressed. Chapter 8 considers the ways in which authors' texts and the teacher can facilitate students' development of their storymaking abilities.

## Special Features

In addition to the different types of print used to indicate various voices, several other features are included. At the beginning of each chapter, an overview is provided. In the analysis of events, lines are used to mark off where transcripts begin and end. At the end of each chapter is a section entitled Bridging Theory into Practice. In these sections, conclusions lead to questions regarding authors' texts and storymaking processes in the classroom. Groups of questions are marked by bullets as are other sections in the chapter where they might be useful.

## ACKNOWLEDGMENTS

I acknowledge the teachers and students who have opened their classrooms to me. Several teachers who have coauthored and copresented with me, Donna Canan, Elaine Handloff, and Annyce Gerber (Meiners), are referred to by their first names in this volume. Other teachers who participated in studies but prefer pseudonyms are Denise, Lena, Marsha, and Vivian. A special thanks goes to all these committed professionals.

In addition, I thank Beverly McLain for her help in the preparation of the manuscript.

—*Joanne M. Golden*

# I

# SOCIAL SEMIOTICS AND CLASSROOM TEXTS

# 1

# Storymaking
# in the Classroom

In this chapter, classrooms are considered as unique contexts for storymaking processes. Texts are selected for particular reasons; interactions among participants are structured for particular outcomes; and abilities in constructing and interpreting stories are assessed. A social semiotic perspective offers a way of looking at how meaning evolves when texts are embedded in classroom discourse.

*Dear Karen,*

*My name is Shala … I am enjoying Scorpions. Are you? What do you think about Jamal? I think he is very confused. He can't figure out what he wants to do. Stay in the gang or earn money honestly. Jamal needs a friend who will help him find out what is right or wrong. Jamal should tell Abuela the truth about the gun. But I know it's easier said, than done … I can't wait to find out about Randy … I am wondering if Abuela will let Tito come back home to stay. I am trying to guess what might happen in Chapter 13. I think maybe Mr. Gonzalez's store might get robbed by the Scorpions. The Scorpions may try to get Jamal to take the money while he's working their.*

Shala, a seventh-grader in an inner-city alternative school, wrote this letter to a preservice teacher who had read Walter Dean Myers' (1988) novel *Scorpions* in her college class. Her letter conveys the different ways she engaged with the text: interpreting the character's confusion, observing what he

**3**

needs, and prescribing what he should do. Shala is motivated to find out about Jamal's brother Randy and wonders if Tito's grandmother will take him back. She predicts the gang will rob the store while Jamal is working there. In addition to constructing, predicting, and interpreting text, Shala communicates her enjoyment of the novel.

In her class's unit on the novel, Shala orally interpreted textual passages and listened to classmates read sections of the novel aloud. She participated in literature circle discussions by interpreting the text, connecting it to her life and the world, identifying significant passages, and illustrating a memorable scene. She wrote a letter of advice to the main character, speculated on what she would do in his position, and conveyed her view of the author's message. In addition, Shala compared the theme of friendship in *Scorpions* and Rosa Guy's (1974) novel, *The Friends*.

This example from Donna's seventh-grade class illustrates how classrooms are arenas for storymaking events in which participants transform an array of phonemic, graphic, and iconic cues into meaningful works. Like homes, community groups, workplaces, and many other social contexts, classrooms are special places where humans interact with texts and each other to make meaning. Like other communicative contexts, classrooms involve "complex interrelationships of semiotic systems comprising structures and codes for making meaning" (Hodge & Kress, 1988, p. 2).

## CLASSROOMS ARE UNIQUE SEMIOTIC SYSTEMS

A major goal of schools is to develop students' abilities to make meaning through texts in a variety of situations. This requires engaging students in a range of literacy practices, often reflecting "talk-around texts" (Barton, 1994). These literacy practices are governed by rules and expectations, which are influenced by mainstream cultural values.

As educational systems, classrooms function as "transformational processes that produce social beings for society" (Hodge & Kress, 1988, pp. 240–241). In this way, they control "the correct form of the production and reproduction of cultural meaning" (p. 249). The power of the classroom in this capacity is evident in the nature of text events. This is reflected in text practices, texts in use, text channels, intertexts, participants' roles, and assessment of students.

### Text Practices

The teacher's instructional goals influence the nature of the text event, including the choice of texts, the rules governing meaning-making, and the ways in which the participants interact in the classroom. How goals are interpreted and acted on in each classroom is influenced by the teacher's attitudes, values, and beliefs regarding meaning-making processes

In Donna's seventh-grade class, which is based on the Paidaia Program, one of her goals is to engage her students in critical thinking through interactions with stimulating texts. She uses essays, poetry, short stories, plays, and other genres. Seminars are structured to evoke an active dialogue among the participants. Like other teachers, her goals for meaning-making are visible in ways that often are implicit in other contexts. Expectations pertaining to procedures, rules for participation, and assessment are communicated to the students.

## Texts in Use

The classroom is unique among other contexts in terms of which texts are used. Imaginative stories, historical accounts, biographies, speeches, math problems, poetry, and scientific records are among the texts in use. Embedded in each text is a network of conventions that govern how it is constructed and interpreted. A story text, for example, is conveyed by a narrator and comprises a cast of characters enacting and reacting to other characters and events, which are situated in time and space. These features are evident in the following summary of key events in *Scorpions*:

> Randy's older brother is in jail, and Jamal is pressured to take his place in the gang, Scorpions, and to raise money to hire a lawyer for his brother. He accepts a gun from one of the gang members. After Jamal is bullied repeatedly by Dwayne, he takes a gun to school against his best friend Tito's advice and pulls it on Dwayne. When word of the incident spreads, Tito hides the gun at his house. His grandmother, Abuela, turns him out of the house when she finds it. At Jamal's request, Tito sneaks back in to retrieve the gun. Jamal's job at Mr. Gonzalez's store is short-lived after gang members threaten him in the store. Jamal meets with his challengers, Angel and Indian, in the park. Tito, agreeing to watch from a distance, shoots both gang members when one pulls a knife on Jamal. In the end, Randy's friend Mack takes over the gang; Tito and Abuela return to Puerto Rico; and Jamal's future remains uncertain.

A narrator introduces the characters Jamal and his family, Tito and Abuela, gang members, classmates, and the principal, among others. The characters also are revealed through their speech, actions, and perception of other characters. A chain of causally connected events is initiated when Jamal accepts the gun from Mack and pulls it on Dwayne. Tito, who cautions Jamal about the dangers of the gun, agrees to hide the gun and later uses it to kill two gang members. Time is confined to a fairly brief period, with occasional flashbacks to provide background information, such as

Jamal's relationship with his father. Events occur in an inner-city setting, shifting between the homes of Jamal and Tito, the school, the boatyard, the park, and the gang's hangout.

## Text Channels

Texts are channeled through oral, written, and visual modes. Stories are experienced through storytelling, reading aloud, dramatizing, film viewing, listening to recordings, and other modes. Interpreting stories, then, requires both knowledge of narrative conventions and knowledge of oral, written, and visual symbols.

Scorpions was experienced in various ways in Donna's class. Donna read the first chapter aloud. Other chapters were interpreted orally by students or read independently. During the oral read-alouds, students listened to the author's text as well as the reader's paralanguage cues. In the film adaptation of Scorpions, viewers' interpretations are influenced by choice of actors, their use of paralanguage, camera shots, sound effects, the musical score, and scenery.

## Intertexts

In classrooms, intertextual links are evident in the connections between the texts of one author, the texts of different authors, and the instructional and interpretive texts that accompany the authors' texts. Scorpions is an example of a narrative text in which a teller conveys information about how characters enact and react to events ordered in time and space. It also is an instance of a particular genre of narrative texts, contemporary realism, in which the story events could occur in the real world. Scorpions can be linked to other authors' works with settings in urban areas such as Jerry Spinelli's (1990) Maniac McGee, themes of gang pressures including Paula Fox's (1967) How Many Miles to Babylon, or a focus on friendship, such as The Friends. Connections also exist with other culturally specific novels featuring African American characters, including those written by Virginia Hamilton, Mildred Pitt Taylor, and Eloise Greenfield. Scorpions is linked also to other novels for middle school readers written by Walter Dean Myers, including Fast Sam, Cool Clyde and Stuff, and Motown and Didi. In addition, Myers' novels are a part of his family of texts, including poetry, biographies, and historical accounts.

Other intertexts that accompany Myers' text are related to instructional processes as reflected in the Donna's talk about the text, her students' discussion in literature circles, and the student's written and visual responses to the text. Other instructional materials and research related to Scorpions appear in various publications. Additional intertexts include Walter Dean Myers' commentaries in speeches, interviews, and essays, as well as critics' reviews of his books.

## Participants' Roles

Classrooms are unique meaning-making enterprises considering the nature of the participants and the relationship among them. Texts in a classroom setting are embedded in a social discourse in which participants interact with the text and each other to construct meaning and significance. This social discourse is characterized by rules and expectations that shape how texts are viewed, how meaning is constructed, and how successful interactions are defined.

In Donna's classroom, students participated in literature circle discussions of *Scorpions*. Mitch assumed the role of connector in his discussion group. One question he posed to his group was, "Place yourself in Jamal's place. Would you have kept the gun?" Tina and Alden agreed that they would not have kept the gun because of the possibility of getting into trouble. Shannah, however, said she would have kept the gun for protection (see the transcript in chap. 4). As this example shows, an individual's interpretations are tested against those of other participants and are confirmed, disconfirmed, modified, and/or extended. In classroom settings, then, works are constructed and interpreted within a community of meaning-makers.

## Assessment of Students

In line with their function of developing textual abilities, classrooms also are distinctive in their systems of monitoring students' success as meaning-makers. Success is determined, in part, by how effectively students respond to the social expectations associated with the text event. For students to perform well in their encounters with text, they must know and apply contextual as well as textual rules for interpretation.

Many students in Donna's class performed their roles in the literature circle discussions according to expectations associated with each role while also observing interactional rules pertaining to participation in a group. However, a student may be well versed in applying textual rules, yet perform poorly as a result of violating social rules. Janet, for example, had prepared questions reflecting her understanding of the text, but during group discussion, she put her head down on the table, declining to interact with others. Conversely, a student may mask a difficulty in constructing and interpreting works by being adept in social processes.

Evaluating students' talk is one of many ways to assess their abilities to construct and interpret text. In Donna's unit on *Scorpions*, she also learned about how her students responded by reading their essay responses at the end of the unit, their charts on how characters are revealed, their classroom mural, and their letters to preservice teachers.

## CLASSROOMS ARE VARIANT SEMIOTIC SYSTEMS

Although classrooms resemble each other in terms of their instructional goals, relationships among text and student and teacher participants, and assessment of meaning-making capabilities, they vary in terms of how these goals are translated into practice. This is evident when the assumptions regarding meaning-making are identified in classroom practices. For example, classrooms contrast in terms of which authors' texts are highlighted and the weight given to the author's words and the contributions of the reader. Certain texts are foregrounded, labeled, and valued. If a valued text is too difficult, it is modified to suit a particular reading level. If it is potentially controversial, it also is adapted so that it conforms to publishers' constraints.

Classrooms also differ in terms of teachers' perceptions of story meaning. Some teachers subscribe to the view that there is a correct interpretation in the author's text to be retrieved, whereas others view texts as generating multiple, defensible meanings.

For example, a teacher who adheres to a formalist approach to interpretation would "believe that we can rely on the words to support our one, correct reading, that meaning is centered in the words of the text" (Moore, 1997, p. 30). Therefore, certain voices (i.e., those of the critic and the teacher) are perceived as the authority for interpretation and accorded a higher status than others. The voice of the critic, reinforced by the teacher, then, is legitimized. An alternative view posited by deconstructionists is that "there is no correct reading."

It is evident from the discussion thus far that the teacher functions prominently in textual practices. She designates the authors' texts or the procedures for selecting them, establishes the framework used to socialize students into ways of interacting and ways of meaning, monitors textual practices, and sanctions students' responses to text. In this way, the classroom parallels the home environment in which children are socialized into a culture, ways of using language, and ways of meaning. Ostensibly, the goal in many classrooms is to induct students into the mainstream culture via a school culture embodying its ways with texts.

The teacher functions as a social agent who enforces, and sometimes challenges, the set of rules associated with certain social semiotic behaviors that conform to the particular forms of social organization reflecting dominant and resistant structures (Hodge & Kress, 1988, pp. 2–3). At the same time, school curricula in literacy also are criticized for "artificial" language, a specialized school discourse that is divorced from the "authentic" discourse outside of school.

## WHY STUDY CLASSROOM TEXT EVENTS?

Classrooms are unique in relation to the value they place on texts and the time allotted to textual practices. Stances toward texts, students, and events in classrooms are replete with social, political, and cultural values that have social, linguistic, and cultural consequences. Literature as a social construction is "an ideological machine concerned with legitimacy and control, working through a system that excludes or privileges certain kinds of texts and specific readings and modes of reading" (Hodge, 1990, p. viii). By studying textual practices in classrooms, we can address the following issues:

- how texts are constructed and interpreted
- which texts are privileged over others
- which types of interactions are encouraged
- whose voices are heard in meaning-making events
- what assumptions are held about text–meaning correspondences
- what assessments are used as indicators of textual competence.

The classroom is clearly a rich resource for exploring social and academic expectations associated with the development of students as storymakers. Studying classroom processes enables us to examine critically what counts as storymaking and, by implication, what is valued in preparing students to participate in storymaking processes in society. To address these complex issues, it is useful to focus on the story as a particular kind of sign.

Stories are a valuable source for exploring how texts are transformed into works via discourse processes for some of the following reasons:

- Historically, stories are a key part of curricula as reflected in the value placed on storybook reading at home and in the early grades of school, and on interpreting literature in the secondary school. This valuing has important sociocultural and political implications.
- The texts themselves are value laden, as are the participants' meanings and significances generated from them.

- Because texts generate multiple meanings, stories enable close looks at factors influencing varied meanings, including the author, the reader, the teacher, and the community.
- Because story is situated in classroom events, it can be considered in terms of its aesthetic function "as a lived through experience" (Rosenblatt, 1976), as well as its instructional function in the development of literacy abilities.
- In classrooms, stories often are embedded in a social discourse in which teachers and students visibly interact to meet social and academic requirements of the lesson. Therefore, a focus on these events offers insights into the nature of teacher–student–author interaction in the construction of meaning.

As Hodge and Kress (1988) note:

Because story is so directly tied into specific semiotic contexts, it is more liable to change than other narrative forms ... [Story is also] more precisely and subtly responsive to immediate social forces ... [and therefore] offers the best site for analysing specific social meanings as well as continuities of cultural values over time. (1988, p. 231)

The exploration of socially situated storymaking processes is facilitated by a close examination of the principal contributors in the process: the authors' texts, the student and teacher participants, and the classroom context. Social semiotics provides a theoretical framework for exploring how readers transform authors' texts into stories, a process embedded in a social discourse produced by teacher and students interacting in the construction of social and academic meanings.

## STORYMAKING IN CLASSROOMS:
## A SOCIAL SEMIOTIC FRAMEWORK

Traditional semiotics attends to the structures and codes governing semiotic systems. A *semiotic system*, such as language, is characterized as a potential sign that is actualized into a sign during interaction with a respondent (Peirce, 1932). A *sign*, according to Peirce is "something that stands to someone for something." Multiple interpretations are generated from this potential sign, each contributing a link in an unending chain. Various disciplines enhance our understanding of the language–message systems in the text and the reader's process of actualizing the work, including linguistics, literary theory, and cognitive psychology. However, many of these analyses in their focus on textual features, psychological processes, or both, do not fully take into account the influence of social context on meaning-making.

In contrast, a main focus of social semiotics is the participants' discourse in the social situations wherein the texts are embedded (Hodge & Kress, 1988). A sign includes both a text and the context in which it is understood and evaluated. A "dialogic" relation occurs when the text encounters the discourse, that is, the "framing" or "reactive" text of the participants (Bakhtin, 1986).

In a classroom setting, a reactive text includes, in part, the personal, interpretive, and evaluative reactions of participants. Through social meaning-making practices, such as story events, participants in the interaction "make, use, dispute, and change textual meanings" (Thibault, 1991, p. 16). The value of viewing storymaking from a social semiotic perspective, then, is that it enables us to extend the notion of story to incorporate "contexts, purposes, and agents and their activities as socially organized structures of meaning" (Hodge, 1990, p. viii).

By analyzing authors' texts and readers' reactive texts in classroom events, we can explore both the nature of the text and the social and academic expectations that influence how the stories evolve. The purpose of the next section is to consider in greater detail the author's text and the reading process, the participants' discourse during interaction with each other, and the dialogic relations between text and discourse.

## Authors' Texts and Reading Processes

Texts are "formal objects," whole units of spoken or written communication seen as coherent syntactic and semantic structures that function as the medium of discourse in interpretive events. The text can be described as a potential sign that is realized during reading and, in some cases, during postreading activities such as those of literature discussion groups.

The smallest semiotic forms in the semiotic act are messages that "pass in clusters back and forth between the participants in a semiotic act" (Hodge & Kress, 1988, p. 5). These messages serve as cues that guide participants in constructing and interpreting stories. The author, through the convention of a narrator, presents a series of messages about the story world. These messages provide explicit and implicit information about the story, such as the specific events that transpired, where and when they occurred, and the characters' involvement in the events. Information pertaining to various textual elements, such as character, is distributed along a linear plane. To construct these elements, the reader not only translates but also integrates information from various sources. In Fairclough's (1992) terms, "texts set up positions for interpreting subjects who can make sense of them and are capable of making connections and inferences in accordance with the relevant interpretive principles necessary to generate coherent readings" (p. 84).

In Doris Lessing's (1975) short story, *A Mild Attack of Locusts*, a young woman from the city marries a farmer, and their farm experiences an attack of locusts. Some traits of the character Margaret are revealed in the narrator's statements; Margaret's thoughts, speech, and actions: and other characters' perceptions. We learn from the narrator that Margaret "never had an opinion of her own on matters like the weather" (p. 539) because of her lack of experience. Her thoughts support her uncertainty in a new environment: "Margaret was wondering what she could do to help. She did not know" (p. 541). When her husband approached her, covered with locusts, Margaret shuddered and exclaimed, "How can you bear to let them touch you?" (p. 543). Her question engendered a look of disapproval from her husband. Her actions in response to the attack of locusts reflect both her frustration and her impulse to hide it from the men: "Margaret roused herself, wiped her eyes, pretended she had not been crying and fetched them some supper" (p. 544). These textual messages show how Margaret is revealed through her actions, thoughts, and speech as well as through the narrator and other characters' perceptions.

Although explicit information about textual elements is supplied by the author, some information requires readers to fill in the gaps or blank spaces. Consequently, a story comprises not only what is said, but also what is not said. Gaps are evident in the form of missing links that connect the story elements (Iser, 1978). In *A Mild Attack of Locusts*, for example, the reader discovers from the narrator that Margaret felt "humbled" when her husband took a first look at "her city self" now attired in the clothes of a proper farmer's wife. Here we can infer that her actions and reactions are explained by her move from the city to a farm. Thus, the reader connects the textual elements of narrator, character, and plot.

This linking of elements sets up another key reader activity: prediction. The reader anticipates that Margaret may not be able to adapt to her new married life. After all, she thought things were "all so hopeless—if it wasn't a bad season, it was locusts; if it wasn't locusts, it was army-worm or veldt fires" (p. 543). This prediction is challenged later when the reader learns that "she was trying to get used to the idea of three or four years of locusts" (p. 544).

A text is never fully translatable because there is no single, correct story that grows out of the reader's interaction with the author's text. Theoretically, a text generates an endless proliferation of stories seen in relationship to each other (Peirce, 1932). This indeterminancy of meaning is attributable to factors related to the text (e.g., implicit information), the reader (e.g., prior knowledge), and the context (e.g., expectations for "doing text" in a particular situation).

However, although texts spawn multiple meanings, stories also generate commonalities in interpretations. Convergence in stories reflects agreement in the "facts," such as events that happened. For example, Golden and Guthrie (1986) found that 98% of a class of ninth-grade readers agreed on the key events in Jessamyn West's (1943) short story, *Reverdy*, as well as the order in which they occurred. In-common readings also may arise from a particular community of readers who share a similar knowledge of textual and interpretive conventions (Fish, 1980).

The "facts" of the story also can lead to divergent interpretations, some more plausible than others (de Beaugrande, 1980). Implausible interpretations, for example, can result from misreadings of the information (e.g., by replacing one word with a nonsynonymous word, omitting a key detail, reading a statement literally vs. figuratively). Divergent interpretations also reflect variation in the reader's affective responses. Golden and Guthrie (1986) found a significant correlation between the ninth graders' interpretation of theme and their empathy for a particular character. That is, readers empathetic to the character *Reverdy* chose a theme associated with *Reverdy*, whereas readers who empathized with the narrator identified a theme related to the narrator.

Although an author's cues evoke similar cognitive activities among readers and produce convergent constructions, readers do not merely assemble a work. Each reader is actively and uniquely involved as a co-creator of the work, drawing on the textual repertoire and filling in the unwritten parts of the story. In addition, the knowledge, attitudes, beliefs, and experiences that readers bring to the act of storymaking influence the nature of the story that evolves (Ortony, 1985; van Dijk & Kintsch, 1983). This prior "theory of the world" is shaped by factors associated with the individual reader as well as by factors associated with his or her sociocultural community.

Furthermore, the role of the reader is not limited to the construction and interpretation of a text. The reader also plays a role in determining the significance of the story. Significance can be construed in terms of the effect the story has on the reader (Iser, 1978). This effect is evident in various ways, depending on the nature of the text and the goals of the reader. Significance can be ascertained, for example, in terms of how the text stimulates the reader to look at self or everyday life in a new way.

## Discourse: Interaction Among Participants

*Text*, "a structure of messages which has a socially ascribed unity" (Hodge & Kress, 1988, p. 5), is embedded in a social discourse wherein participants interact to generate meaning. Therefore, the requisite aspects of a social semiotic theory of language are the text, the means of exchange, and the situation, all part of the interactive process in which meanings are exchanged (Halliday, 1978).

In Bakhtin's (1986) view, any utterances positioned alongside one another on the same semantic plane enter into a dialogic relation. When an individual responds to a given utterance, he or she participates in a dialogue and, in so doing, influences how the utterance is understood. Bakhtin described the text of the respondent (e.g., the reactive text) as one that comments on, evaluates, answers questions, and so forth in relation to the utterance. In this way, a series of rejoinders to an utterance contributes to the dialogic chain.

A segment from a small group discussion of *A Mild Attack of Locusts* among four eighth graders and their teacher illustrates the dialogic relation between text and discourse. In the following segment, the relevant information presented in Lessing's (1975) text precedes the participants' related discourse:

> She felt suitably humble—just as she had when he had first taken a look at her city self, hair waved and golden, nails red and pointed. (p. 543)

| | |
|---|---|
| Teacher: | *What about the characters, particularly Margaret, the main character?* |
| Doug: | *Yeah, Margaret, the city girl.* |
| Ben: | *The city girl, right. It was one of those weird hairdos … the people had.* |
| Jan: | *The picture with the hair up. I picture her as a young girl that was kind of like married off.* |
| Teacher: | *Uh. humm.* |
| Ben: | *Yeah.* |

> She never had an opinion of her own on matters like the weather, because even to know about what seems a simple thing like the weather needs experience. Which Margaret had not got. (p. 539)

| | |
|---|---|
| Jan: | *And was willing to do anything. That bugged me a lot.* |
| Peter: | *I pictured her as young, but she really wasn't that young.* |
| Teacher: | *She wasn't all that young. What bugged you about her?* |
| Jan: | *The fact that she was willing to do just about anything.* |
| Teacher: | *Just about anything?* |

| Jan:     | *That she didn't have an opinion about the weather ... Right, that bugged me.* |
|----------|----------------------------------------------------------------------|
| Teacher: | *Yeah, she was very passive, yeah right.* |
| Peter:   | *No women's lib; you don't like the story—that's the only reason you don't like the story?* |
| Jan:     | *Well, it just bugged me—I liked the story.* |
| Peter:   | *Well, that's how it was.* |

Jan's comments reflect her view that Margaret is a character who does not have a strong will. That is, she is willing to do anything, and she does not have an opinion of her own. In a later part of the discussion, Jan continued to interpret Margaret as a weak character who did not "choose" to become more knowledgeable. Other participants, including the teacher and Peter, constructed a different view of the character as inexperienced with farm life, yet willing to be helpful. As a result of the dialogue, Jan seemed to modify her judgment of Margaret, as illustrated in her following comment:

> I pictured him older and her younger because she sounded kind of like unexperienced and not really knowing what she was doing and it was really because she had never been there, but it just gave me the impression that she was young and was kind of wimpish.

These exchanges about the character suggest that multiple interpretations are possible and that participants through discourse can influence how other participants perceive aspects of the story world. In this way, a dialogic relation occurs between the author's words and the participants' discourse.

*Discourse* is the "process of linguistic interaction between people uttering and comprehending texts" (Fowler, 1996, p. 111). Discourse concerns how participants act in situations and how they relate interpersonally. In Halliday's (1978) view, it is this interpersonal function of language that connects texts with context. Moreover, it is this function that links text and discourse.

## Context: Classroom Events

Like text, social context is constructed by participants, and meaning is indeterminate and unbounded, continuously open to confirmation and modification. Texts always occur in a context, and rules and expectations governing meaning construction affect the dialogic relation between text and discourse. Thibault (1991) observed that "texts and the relations among voices in textual practice are constantly recontextualized in and through the dialogic interactions between social discourses" (pp. 121–122).

Classroom events, like story texts, also are socially and culturally coded and rule-bound. We read the participants' talk to construct the social text that "flows" alongside the author's text and the dialogic relation between the author's text and the social text. Attitudes, values, beliefs, and practices regarding "doing story" in classrooms are visibly discernible when we examine the nature of the exchange among participants and the kind of reactive text that evolves.

Lemke (1990) argued in his sociosemiotic analyses of science lessons that "talking science" is a social process in which a community of people who share certain attitudes, beliefs, and values is formed. Teaching science, therefore, involves not just a mastery of knowledge and skills, but also participation in a community of people who "talk science." Similarly, the use of story in classrooms offers great potential for understanding how societies reproduce their value systems because they are so centrally tied into "specific semiosic contexts" as well as cultural value systems over time (Hodge & Kress, 1988, p. 231).

The teacher is a key creator of the social text in her role of transmitting the valued sociocultural ways of storymaking. Academic values are evident in several ways. First, the selection of the text reflects a certain value judgment based on the purpose of the lesson, the preferences of the students, and the quality of the literature (e.g., whether it is an award winner). Second, the teacher determines the nature of the dialogic relationship between participants and story text in his or her focus on how to "read" the information, how to construct a story world, and how to find significance between self and story. In each case, the teacher conveys a message to the students about the function of story text. In response, students must take up the role of "reading" the teacher's as well as the author's words. The student successfully meets the academic demands of the event if he or she conforms to the teacher's expectations for academic participation.

In addition to the academic expectations in discourse, there are the social expectations for participating in a group. With reference to social expectations, teachers and students interact in culturally patterned ways learned through participation in discourse processes (Green & Smith, 1983). These patterned or rule-governed ways of interacting include such processes as gaining access to conversations, turn taking, and interacting in socially acceptable ways. Expectations for participation vary depending on "the communicative requirements of the situation, the nature of the activity, and/or the goal of the activity" (Green & Smith, 1983). In classroom events, teachers are central in structuring the lesson and in establishing expectations for participation. They design the communicative task framework, such as class members' construction and interpretation of a text. Through this framework "teacher–student interaction mediates how students interpret what they are about and what it means" (Bloome, 1987, p. 139).

The result of the social process of constructing meaning may support the reader in clarifying, extending and adjusting (in the case of misreading) his or her interpretation. However, the contextual demands for meaning-making may also inhibit this process when participants are required to bridge between conflicting sets of expectations about storymaking. For example, storymaking in a reader's cultural community, as shown in studies on narratives, may clash with expectations for doing text in the reader's school community (Cook-Gumperz, 1986; Heath, 1983; Michaels, 1981).

The teacher's way of conducting discourse may be influenced by other more indirect influences, which should be acknowledged in the analysis. The choices of texts and the nature of the interactions among participants, for example, can be affected by expectations from curriculum designers, administrators, school and/or district guidelines, and community pressures. When the teacher and students are participants in a research project, the investigator's expectations affect the discourse.

In the discussion involving *A Mild Attack of Locusts*, the teacher and students were participants in a study exploring how readers make meaning of stories (Golden, 1986). The setting was the eighth-grade classroom (comprising nine students) in an alternative school whose purpose was to promote creative learning. The teacher was asked to serve as a facilitator and as a coparticipant in the discussion whose purpose was "to make sense out of the story."

Analysis of the discourse accompanying the text, then, helps us to understand the challenges some readers encounter when meeting the social and academic demands of storymaking.

## BRIDGING THEORY INTO PRACTICE

In this chapter, a social semiotic perspective is presented as a way of exploring the nature of storymaking processes in educational settings. This perspective offers an opportunity for looking closely at the processes involved in transforming authors' texts into stories. The role of discourse in text practices, the relationship among participants, the choice and mode of text, and the assessment of students' responses are identified as important aspects of storymaking.

In reviewing the nature of text in context identified in this chapter, consider how text practices transpire in a particular classroom. Then think about the implications of these practices for students' enjoyment of texts and the development of their abilities to construct and interpret stories.

- Consider how the authors' texts are selected for classroom use.

    Who chooses the texts?
    Why are particular texts emphasized?
    What will students learn from engaging with these texts?

- Consider the kinds of discourse in which the authors' texts are embedded.

    What are the different ways in which students talk about texts?
    What is the role of the teacher and that of the students in the discussion?
    How do students interact with each other to build stories?
    In addition to talk, what kinds of responses to texts are encouraged?

- Consider the different channels in which authors' texts appear.

    Do students read texts independently?
    Do students read authors' texts during and outside of class?
    Are texts read aloud by the teacher, the students, or both?
    Are texts experienced in written, oral, and visual forms?

- Consider the ways in which texts are connected to other texts.

    Do students learn about other texts written by an author?
    Do they see the authors' texts in the context of other authors' texts?
    Do they see texts produced by others in response to the authors' texts?

- Consider the ways in which students' responses to authors' texts are assessed.

    What counts as evidence of students' storymaking abilities?
    Are particular indices more informative than others?
    How is development of students' abilities assessed?

# 2

## The Author's Text

In this chapter, authors' and illustrators' guides to the reader for constructing and interpreting characters, time relations, and position of the narrators are explored. Close readings of particular texts are used to illustrate how the authors' words, the illustrators' pictures, and the readers' oral interpretation facilitate the storymaking process. Examples also indicate how alteration of the cue systems in adaptations can influence the storymaking process.

Specific cues in the author's text guide the reader in constructing, interpreting, and signifying story. These cues point to narrative elements of setting, plot, character narrator, and theme, among others. This chapter focuses on the author's cues for building three central narrative elements: character, time, and narrator (Rimmon-Kenan, 1983). Several texts including a novel, a picture storybook, a storybook reading event, and adaptations of texts serve as the basis for examining these elements.

An author's text is articulated in a string of symbols arranged linearly. The author's selection and arrangement of these symbols are governed by semiotic codes pertaining to language, society, and culture as well as by the author's individual style. Because of the indeterminate nature of the author's work, multiple meanings can be generated from it both by the same and by different readers (Iser, 1978). The transformation of a text into a story is played out on a "methodological field," which is animated through the interpreter's activity (Barthes, 1979, p. 74). How readers act on an author's text and respond to it depends, in part, on their knowledge of linguistic structures and conventions of narrative texts, as well as their ability to apply textual strategies, such as predicting and inferencing.

## TEXTUAL CUES

To view the contributions of the author's text in the construction of the narrative, it is important to identify cues that give rise to the story world. A narrative is a textual world conveyed by a narrator in which characters enact and react to a series of events bounded by time and space. The author selects and orders cues for constructing characters, time, and narrator(s) to reflect culturally sanctioned narrative conventions (which may vary across cultures), as well as the author's individual style of writing.

Information pertaining to narrative elements is strewn along the linear path. To formulate each element, the reader identifies, translates, and connects this information and fills in the unwritten parts of the narrative. To construct a character, the reader identifies, infers, and integrates traits to assemble the character's profile. To construct time, the reader identifies events in terms of when they happened, how long they lasted, and how often they occurred. To construct the narrator, the reader identifies the narrator(s) telling the story and the perspective from which the story is told. A story world emerges when the reader integrates these and other narrative elements such as setting and plot.

In the following section, characters are viewed in terms of the ways in which they are revealed; time is considered according to the dimensions of order, duration, and frequency; and narrator is addressed in terms of perceptibility and focalization (Golden, 1990). Jean Fritz's (1982) novel, *Homesick*, is used to illustrate how textual cues can guide the reader in constructing and connecting the three narrative elements.

## TEXTUAL CUES IN A NOVEL

### Character

In "reading" a character, the reader translates, inferences, and integrates information to form a tentative profile, which is confirmed, modified, or abandoned as new data are encountered. Relevant information is revealed through different sources including the narrator, other characters, and the character's speech, actions, and thoughts. In some cases, information from different sources is compatible, whereas in other cases, there is conflict. For example, a character may see him or herself differently from the way other characters do.

To illustrate information pertaining to character, excerpts from the first chapter of Fritz's (1982) *Homesick* follow with the sources noted in parentheses. After Jean, the narrator, refuses to sing the British national anthem at her school in China because she is American, another character threatens her at recess:

"You wouldn't sing it. So say it," he ordered. (speech) "Let me hear you say it." (speech) I tried to pull my foot away but he only ground down harder. (actions) "Say what?" (speech) I was telling my face please not to show what my foot felt. (thought) "God save the king. Say it. Those four words. I want to hear you say it." (speech) Although Ian Forbes was short, he was solid and tough and built for fighting ... So it was crazy for me to argue with him. (narrator) "Why should I?" I asked. "Americans haven't said that since George the Third." (speech) He grabbed my right arm and twisted it behind my back. (actions) "Say it," he hissed. (speech) I felt the tears come to my eyes and I hated myself for the tears.... (thought) "I'll never say it," I whispered. (p. 12).... I flung myself on the bed. What was there to think? Either I went to school and got beaten up. Or I quit ... (thought) My mother shook her head. (action) Yes, it was simple, she agreed. I could go back to the British School, be sensible, and start singing about the king again. (other's perceptions) (p. 27)

In these brief passages, several traits of both Jean and Ian are revealed. Ian's speech and actions show that he is a bully who appears to be loyal to his country (e.g., his actions imply that he thinks everyone should sing his national anthem). He is persistent in his goal of making Jean sing and uses speech (threat) and physical force (action) to achieve his goal. Jean's actions and speech indicate that she is determined and loyal to America (which is also evident in previous passages). As her thoughts reveal, it seems that her outward bravado masks her fear of Ian. (This is later confirmed in her act of skipping school to avoid him as well as singing the anthem.) The passage also suggests that Jean has some knowledge of history, as implied by her reference to King George the Third.

Therefore, in two brief passages at the beginning of the novel, the reader encounters information that provides some basis for formulating tentative traits of Jean, which subsequently can be confirmed, modified, or abandoned as new traits are introduced. In conjunction with the author's information, the reader will write the unwritten parts of the story and engage in interpretive processes, all of which will contribute to the construction of the characters.

## Time

Time focuses on the organization of events in the story. Time can be viewed according to order, duration, and frequency of events (Genette, 1980). In terms of *order*, the occurrence of story events can correspond with the place where they occur in the narrative, as in the case of a straight chronology. Events can happen before they are narrated, as when the narrator recalls a past event (i.e., an analepse), or they can be narrated before their occurrence, as when a narrator looks ahead to an event that has not happened (i.e., prolepse). Genette (1980) observed that prolepses are more common in first-person narratives, in which the retrospective narrator can allude to events in the future that already are a part of the past.

*Duration* concerns the amount of time an event takes in relation to the length of text allotted to narrating. In summaries, for example, the narration is shorter than what has happened (e.g., "a hundred years passed"). In dream sequences, narration time is longer than the story events, and in scenes with actions of short duration and dialogues, story event and narration time are equal.

*Frequency* refers to how often an event has occurred including once; more than once, but told once; and repeatedly, or told more than once. In the following passage from *Homesick*, information related to time is placed in parentheses:

> It would be almost two years before we'd go to America. I was ten years old now. I'd be twelve then. (order) But how could I think about years? (duration) I didn't even dare to think about the next day. (order) After school I ran all the way home, fast so I couldn't think at all…. (order) "I'm home!" I yelled. Then I remembered that it was Tuesday, the day my mother taught an English class at the Y.M.C.A. where my father was the director. (order) … Once I asked my best friend, Andrea, if the hall made her feel little too. (order) She said no. She was going to be a dancer and she loved the space…. (order) Andrea Hull was a year older than I was and knew about everything sooner. (order) She told me about commas, for instance, long before I took punctuation seriously. (order) How could I write letters without commas? she asked. She made me so ashamed that for months I hung little wagging comma-tails all over the letters to my grandmother…. (duration) I wished that Andrea were with me now, but she lived out in the country and I didn't see her often. (frequency) (p. 14)

Several instances of order are evident in the preceding passage, such as when Jean looks ahead to her trip to America and when she comments about her mother working. Duration is apparent when Jean reports that she spent months writing letters with commas. In addition, this action reveals that Jean is influenced by Andrea and what she knows. Frequency is reflected in Jean's comment that she did not see Andrea often. This, in conjunction with her disappointment that her mother is not home, contributes to the reader's sense of Jean's loneliness. In the preceding passage, then, the reader experiences time in the past, present, and future.

## Narration

Two textual dimensions that offer information about the narrator are the perceptibility of the narrator (Chatman, 1978) and the focalization of the narration (Genette, 1980). In terms of *perceptibility*, narrators are oriented toward either the covert or overt end of the continuum. At the covert end, the narrator remains "hidden in the discursive shadows" and is revealed, in part, through expression of characters' speech and thought and in indirect form (Chatman, 1978, p. 196). Overt narrators are indicated through more direct means including descriptions of settings, temporal summaries, reports of what characters did not think or say, and commentaries. *Focalization* refers to the perspective or point of view from which the story is told, that is, by narrators who participate in the events or by those who are outside the events (Genette, 1980).

In first-person narrative, the narrator is overt because the first person is a construct for conveying events from the narrator's own perspective. The following passage from *Homesick* illustrates the presence of the narrator in terms of perceptibility:

> I wasn't going to think about myself. Or Ian Forbes. Or the next day. I wasn't. I wasn't. And I didn't. Not all afternoon. Not all evening. Still, I must have decided what I was going to do because the next morning when I started for school ... (temporal summaries) I walked straight ahead. I wasn't going to school that day. I walked toward the Yangtse River. Past the store that sold paper pellets that opened up into flowers when you dropped them in a glass of water. Then up the block where the beggars sat. (setting description) I never saw anyone give money to a beggar. (commentary) You couldn't, my father explained, or you'd be mobbed by beggars. They'd follow you everyplace; they'd never leave you alone. I had learned not to look at them when I passed and yet I saw. The running sores, the twisted legs, the mangled faces. What I couldn't get over was that, like me, each one of those beggars had only one life to live. It just happened that they had drawn rotten ones. (commentary) (pp. 19–20)

Several cues support the presence of an overt narrator. The reader learns about the passing of time through temporal summaries. This is evident in the first part of the excerpt when the narrator mentions how she did not think about herself the next afternoon and evening. We see her again the next morning. The narrator's presence is indicated also through the use of setting descriptions showing the walk toward the Yangtse River. Finally, the narrator is evident in the commentaries about the appearance and lot of the beggars.

A second aspect of the narrator is *focalization*, the perspective from which the narrative is told, which is not necessarily that of the narrator. In contrast to focalization, voice is the medium through which the story is told to the audience. A third- or first-person voice, for example, can relate the narrative from the point of view of a main character. Genette (1980) identified three types of focalization in narratives: nonfocalized internal, external, and nonfocalized external.

In an internally focalized narrative, the narrator says only what a given character knows. That is, the point of view is that of one character. First-person narratives, such as *Homesick*, exemplify internally focalized narratives. Therefore, events in this book are told by Jean from Jean's perspective.

In the previous excerpts, a range of cues about character, time, and narrator are illustrated with emphasis on the first chapter of *Homesick*. The reader encounters a continuous flow of information pertaining to character, time, and narrator. New information may cause the reader to reject, modify, or confirm constructions. The same information can generate common interpretations. For example, readers can refer to the "facts" of the text to learn what events occurred and the order in which they happened.

In contrast, the same messages can lead various readers to different interpretations. As noted previously, the character Jean was interpreted in this text as knowledgeable, loyal to her country, principled, and fond of her grandmother. Another reader, however, might build an alternative view of Jean as stubborn, conceited, spoiled, and disobedient. Still other views could integrate these dissimilar portraits into a complex character or create a different profile.

In an externally focalized narratives, the narrator says less than the character knows, reflecting an objective report. A character's speech and actions are conveyed rather than his or her thoughts or feelings. An example of this type of narrative is Kjelgaard's (1975) *Blood on the Ice*, which relays how a fox and a bear struggle for survival from both of their perspectives:

The dull eyes of the polar bear could discern only what was beneath his black nose. But his nose told him that the quest must continue. The cold wind that swept in from the north carried no scent of an open land, and therefore there would be no seals. The polar bear sat down, bracing his huge body with his ponderous front paws, and looked behind him.... The little white fox sat 10 feet away. In the gloom his eight-pound, thickly furred body was a warped image that seemed to shimmer into and out of the frozen background. The fox's bushy tail was curled about his hind legs, and the steady wind that whipped out of the north ruffled his fur. (p. 249)

In nonfocalized narratives, an omniscient narrator knows and says more than any one character knows and says as in the case of Hobb's (1989) *Bearstone*:

Walter still had the cast on his leg, and he knew he couldn't negotiate the basement stairs. Wrapped up in a blanket, he sat in a chair at the top of the landing, where he could see the boy down below. He had to content himself with lending know-how and moral support. Cloyd was mixing concrete. He'd carried the hundred-pound bags of cement downstairs himself, as well as countless buckets of sand and gravel, and now he was making concrete. It was chilly in the basement, but as long as he was working, he was warm enough in his denim jacket. He was happy taking care of the old man. He'd grown so used to wandering alone in the canyons, wandering alone in the school corridors, having his own private world. Now he wasn't alone anymore. (pp. 150–151)

Although these examples feature different types of focalization, it is not always easy to determine the focalization of some narratives as in Hamilton's (1982) *Sweet Whispers, Brother Rush*. Moreover, the type of focalization may not be consistent throughout the narrative as in Zindel's (1968) *The Pigman*, wherein two characters alternate the narration. In Wilder's (1953) *Little House in the Big Woods*, focalization changes within chapters from nonfocalized to internally focalized narration:

After supper Pa took Laura and Mary on his knees and said he had a new story to tell them.... When I went to town yesterday with the furs I found it hard walking in the soft snow ... (p. 109)

## TEXTUAL CUES IN A PICTURE
## STORYBOOK

A picture storybook represents a unique channel in which words and pictures and their interrelationships provide the way into the story world. In Barthes' (1977) view, words and pictures form a relay system in which one symbol system anchors the other. To anchor words, pictures function in a variety of ways including specifying, clarifying, and extending information. Conversely, words anchor pictures by focusing attention on relevant aspects of the narrative and by channeling the multiple images present in the pictures. Nodelman (1988) observed that whereas pictures provide information, it is words that focus them: "Reading a picture for narrative meaning is a matter of applying our understanding of words" (p. 211).

Whether pictures show more than what words can say really depends on the relationship between pictures and words in various picture books. Five relationships that predominate in some picture storybooks were identified in Golden (1990): (a) words and pictures are independent (e.g., *The Tale of Peter Rabbit*); (b) pictures are dependent on words (e.g., *Squawk to the Moon; Little Goose*); (c) pictures enhance the story (e.g., *Heckedy Peg*); (d) text carries the primary information (e.g., *The Crane Maiden*); and (e) pictures carry the primary information (e.g., *Rosie's Walk*).

Many storybooks, however, reveal more than one kind of picture–text relationship. The pictures in Kellogg's (1977) *The Mysterious Tadpole*, for example, specify, clarify, and extend information revealed in the words. The pictures provide the humorous connotations by showing that the character, Alphonse, is clearly not a tadpole as he is labeled. His evolving size is humorously depicted when he outgrows the jar, the bathtub, and the school swimming pool. Picture–word relations are described in the following discussion with reference to the different yet complementary cue systems present in *The Mysterious Tadpole*. In considering each element (i.e., character, time, and narrator), the word information is represented on the left side and the picture information on the right.

|  | *Words* | *Pictures* |
|---|---|---|
| Character: | After making sure that Alphonse | Alphonse is in the |
| Actions | felt at home, Louis went to bed. | school swimming |
|  |  | pool and Louis is |
| Time: |  | looking back from |
| Order |  | the steps with the |
|  |  | rug under his arm. |
|  |  | Each is waving. |

In the preceding excerpt, pictures and words interact to convey both Louis's and Alphonse's actions. We infer from the picture that "Alphonse felt at home" because of the size of the swimming pool and his contented expression. We see that Louis is reassured when he looks back from the steps and waves good-bye. Words alone convey that Louis went back to bed. These cues support an interpretation that Louis is very fond of Alphonse and feels a responsibility toward him. Alphonse appears to feel secure about being left alone in the pool.

| | *Words* | *Pictures* |
|---|---|---|
| Character: Thought | Far away in Scotland Uncle McAllister was also thinking about the approaching | The uncle is climbing over rocks with his dog |
| Time: Duration | birthday. While out hiking he discovered an unusual stone in a clump of grass and sticks. | and cat. A smile is on his face as he spots the |
| Character: Action Speech | "A perfect gift for my nephew!" he cried "I'll deliver it in person!" | stone. The stone is large, oval-shaped, and spotted. The lake in the background is bordered by mountains. |

Uncle McAllister's thoughts, actions, and speech are reflected in words, whereas the illustrations provide connotations for the words. From a previous passage, we learned that a year has passed and Louis is thinking about his birthday, as is his uncle. Uncle McAllister appears happy to find an "unusual" stone because he is smiling. It is evident that the uncle likes unusual things, that he is interested in helping Louis with his nature collection, and that he is excited about giving it to him because he delivers it in person. The narrator conveys that the stone is "unusual," and this is specified in the picture by its large, oval-shape, and spotted features.

From the picture, the reader can predict that the stone is an egg that eventually will hatch (and it does as is shown in the last picture of the book). The reader can infer that the uncle likes animals because a dog and a cat accompany him. The rough terrain is conveyed through the words and pictures (e.g., a hilly region with a lake in Scotland). Because the uncle found the Loch Ness monster here, the reader expects him to find another unique gift. In these ways, the pictures function to specify and extend word information. In terms of descriptive detail, more story information is conveyed in the picture than in the words.

|  | Words | Pictures |
|---|---|---|
| Character:<br>Perception<br>Speech | Miss Seevers said, "I'm convinced that your uncle has given you a very rare Loch Ness monster!" | Louis and the librarian are in the library in a section displaying books on lost ships. Her purse is dripping water because she had dropped it in the pool. We infer that she is excited about her theory because she keeps the purse on her arm. She is reading a newspaper entitled *Scientists Search Scotland for the Loch Ness Monster.* |

After a phone conversation with Uncle McAllister, who identifies Alphonse's lake as Loch Ness, Miss Seevers guesses that he is the rare Loch Ness monster. Information from the pictures either confirms or extends this. For example, we see Miss Seevers' look of surprise as she opens the newspaper. The headlines read "Rare Loch Ness Monster," with a photograph that resembles Alphonse. Louis looks on with an interested expression. Miss Seevers and Louis are in a section of the library where books on sunken ships are displayed. Some readers might anticipate that these books will play a role in the story. For an explanation of the dripping purse, the reader must refer to the preceding picture, in which Miss Seevers dropped her purse into the pool when she first encountered Alphonse.

In this example, a number of descriptive details are provided in the pictures rather than in the words. The reader engages in making inferences and predictions to make sense of the text, often on the basis of picture information.

|  | *Words* | *Pictures* |
|---|---|---|
| Character:<br>  Action | Every morning Louis spent<br>several hours swimming with<br>his friend. In the afternoon he | Louis is in the<br>pool tossing<br>cheeseburgers |
| Time:<br>  Frequency | earned the money for<br>Alphonse's cheeseburgers by<br>delivering newspapers. | heaped on a plate<br>into Alphonse's<br>mouth. Both are |
| Time:<br>  Duration |  | smiling. |
| Time:<br>  Order |  |  |

Two actions are conveyed through words: Louis and Alphonse swimming and Louis delivering newspapers. Although the words refer to "swimming," the picture shows Louis and Alphonse in the pool with Louis tossing cheeseburgers into Alphonse's mouth. The reader infers that this is a part of their swimming routine. Their shared pleasure in this activity is expressed in their smiles. The picture extends information about the morning swimming activity, whereas the words provide details not evident in the picture. As noted previously, descriptive versus temporal information is supplied by the pictures. In terms of time, we learn from the words that Louis and Alphonse swim every morning (frequency) for several hours (duration), whereas Louis delivers papers in the afternoon (order).

A picture storybook represents a particular type of text in which words, pictures, and their interrelationships provide the way into the story world. As noted previously, words and pictures form a relay system in which one symbol system anchors the other (Barthes, 1977). To anchor words, pictures function in a variety of ways that include specifying information, clarifying information, extending information, and providing connotations. Words, on the other hand, anchor pictures by focusing attention on relevant aspects of the narrative, that is, by channeling the multiple images present in the picture. In some cases, information is conveyed by the words alone (e.g., temporal relations), whereas in other cases, the picture stands alone (e.g., a bird emerges from the "unusual" stone).

The pictures in *The Mysterious Tadpole* both specify and extend information in the words. The illustrations provide humorous connotations by showing how a preposterous character is accommodated in a semirealistic setting. Setting is conveyed through the school named after Jesse James with figures of James and his guns framing the door. Furthermore, the teacher bars Alphonse from the classroom without investigating his curious nature. She is right that Alphonse is clearly not a tadpole as he is initially labeled.

His visual size accents the humor of the description in words relating that he is growing too big for the jar, the bathtub, and the school swimming pool. The understated language regarding his size emphasizes the incongruity of the situation.

## TEXTUAL CUES IN A STORYBOOK READING EVENT

In the preceding section, *The Mysterious Tadpole* was examined in terms of the nature of two cue systems—author's words and pictures—and the interaction between them. When storybooks are shared during read-aloud events, it is possible to observe which cues participants link into during the story construction process. To explore some of these linkages further, a storybook event involving May, an 8-year-old, and Ana, her 3-year-old sister reading *The Mysterious Tadpole* is examined (Golden & Zuniga-Hill, 1990). Segments from this event reflect some of the primary strategies that May used to scaffold the work for her sister as well as the ways Ana linked into the unfolding text.

From the outset of the event, Ana wanted to match the name of a character to the corresponding figure in the picture. May responded by confirming or correcting her sister's guess. In addition, May substituted her own language for that of the author, on occasion, for the purpose of suiting it to what she perceived to be Ana's level of understanding. To illuminate these patterns in the following segments, the author's words appear in CG Times whereas the participants' exchange is shown in italics. May's alterations of the author's words are in parentheses.

In the following segment, May read about Louis receiving his birthday gift from his Uncle McAllister: a tadpole for his nature collection. In the accompanying picture, a mailman stands in the doorway watching Louis while a neighbor looks on from her door across the hall. Also observing are Louis's parents who are seated at the table by a birthday cake.

May: Uncle McAllister lived in Scotland.
Ana: *Is that? Who? (points to mailman)*
May: *Uh uh. That's Uncle McAllister right there. (points to previous page)* Every year he (Uncle McAllister) sent Louis a birthday gift (present)
Ana: *Is that—is that Lucy?*
May: *That's Louis. This is Louis, okay?*
Every year he (Uncle McAllister) sent Louis a birthday gift

*(present)* **for his nature collection.** *Nature collections are like rocks and frogs and stuff like that.*

Ana:      *mmm*

May:      *And ... mm ...* **"This is the best one yet** *(I've ever got)!"* **cried** *(said)* **Louis.** *That's Louis right there.*

Ana's principal interest was in connecting the words associated with the characters of the mailman and Louis to their representations in the pictures. When May took on the role of narrating the story, she altered the words to facilitate Ana's understanding. For example, she changed the original word "gift" to the word "present" and the phrase structure "one yet" to "I've ever got." May defined the concept of the "nature collection," as "rocks and frogs and stuff like that." Ana nodded her understanding.

In a second segment, the story focuses on Alphonse growing too large for the sink and eventually the bathtub. The picture shows Alphonse leaning out of the sink, dishes falling from the sink to the floor, snow outside the window, and a calendar marked January. Louis and his parents are eating at the table and watching Alphonse drip water on the floor. Only Louis is smiling. A plate of cheeseburgers is on a side table.

The next page shows Alphonse hanging over the bathtub, water dripping on the floor. Louis again is smiling as he stands in a puddle of water. His parents, however, are not as amused. The mother carries a stack of cheeseburgers on a plate. Five other empty plates are on the floor. An empty mason jar is next to the tub underscoring Alphonse's growing size. Louis's father is brushing his teeth.

May:      **When Alphonse became too big for his jar,** *Cuz remember, he put him in a jar?* **When Alphonse became too big for his jar, Louis moved him** *(in)* **to the sink.** *See him put his frog in the sink?*

Ana:      *Oh*

May:      *And there are all the cheeseburgers he's gonna eat for dinner, see?*

Ana:      *mmm*

May:      **After Alphonse out-grew** *(got too big for)* **the sink, Louis's parents agreed to let him use** *(said they could let him stay in)* **the bathtub.** *See, he's in the bathtub. He's making a big mess, huh?*

May interrupted her reading of the text to help Ana link into a previous and related passage (time: order). She drew Ana's attention to the illustrations as a way of specifying the author's words, pointing to the pictures and saying, "see?" For example, she pointed to the picture of the "frog" in the sink and then to all the cheeseburgers he will eat. The same pattern occurred when May referred Ana to the picture of Alphonse in the bathtub, interpreting him as "making a big mess, huh?"

A similar strategy is evident in the third segment, in which May altered the author's words and also answered her questions about characters in the picture. In this picture, discussed previously in the chapter, Louis makes sure Alphonse is comfortable in the pool and goes home carrying the rug. Alphonse waves goodbye.

| | |
|---|---|
| May: | **Louis hid Alphonse under a** (*big*) **rug and smuggled him into the school** (*and put him into the swimming pool*). **After making sure that Alphonse felt at home, Louis went back to bed** (*After Louis was sure that Alfonso felt okay, he left*). **Every morning Louis spent several** (*many*) **hours swimming with his friend** (*Alphonse*). **In the afternoon** |
| Ana: | *Is that Alphonse?* |
| May: | *Uh huh. In the afternoon* |
| Ana: | *And what are … ?* |
| May: | *Uh, Louis.* **Every morning Louis spent several hours swimming with his friend** (*spent a lot of time swimming with his friend, Alphonse*). **In the afternoon** |
| Ana: | *Is that Alphonse?* |
| May: | *Uh huh.* **In the afternoon he earned the money for Alphonse's cheeseburgers by delivering newspapers** (*by giving people their papers*). |
| Ana: | *Is that Alphonse … to give papers?* |
| May: | *Louis gives people their papers, and Alphonse eats the cheeseburgers that Louis buys for him.* |

Two patterns apparent in previous exchanges are also evident in this segment. In assuming the role of teller (reader) of the tale, May altered various words of the author in adjusting to her perception of her sister's level. For example, she restated "smuggled," "sure," "several," and "delivering." In response to Ana's question, May confirmed that a picture depicts Alphonse. At the end, May summarized the information in the preceding episode for Ana because she seemed to have some difficulty in processing it.

The preceding segments show how May restated the author's words and elaborated information to make the text more accessible to Ana. Linking word information to picture information was important to both sisters, although May's focus on this seemed to be in response to Ana's interest.

## ALTERING TEXTS FOR INSTRUCTIONAL PURPOSES

One source of authors' texts in many classroom settings are basals or anthologies. Authors' texts from these sources may be altered from the originals in several ways. First, language from the original may be modified to simplify the sentence patterns and word choices. Second, information from the original may be deleted. Third, information may be repositioned when picture–word relationships are changed. These types of changes can affect not only readers' processes of constructing and interpreting text (Davison, 1984; Liebling, 1989), but also their enjoyment (Goodman, 1987).

In the following analyses, a picture storybook and its adapted version and a novel and its adapted version are both compared for the purpose of exploring how the alterations might affect the reader's construction and enjoyment of the texts.

### Swimmy and Its Adapted Version

A comparison of the original, *Swimmy* (Lionni, 1964) and its version (Lionni, 1989) in a basal reader revealed three types of alterations of words and pictures: (a) information reduction in both words and pictures wherein information is deleted from the original, (b) omission of pictures, and (c) alteration of the positioning of words in relation to pictures so that correspondence between words and pictures is changed. In the segments that follow, the underlined portions of the original text in the left column indicate which words were deleted in the adapted version, which appears in the right column.

*a. Information Reduction*

| *Original Words* | *Adapted Words* |
|---|---|
| One bad day a tuna fish, <u>swift fierce, and very hungry came darting through the waves. In one gulp,</u> he swallowed all the little red fish.Only Swimmy escaped. | One bad day a tuna fish came. He swallowed all the little red fish. Only Swimmy escaped. |

| *Original Picture* | *Adapted Picture* |
|---|---|
| A large tuna nearly fills a double-page spread. | The eye and mouth of a tuna are positioned on the left side of a single page. |

As seen in the preceding examples, the original language, which helps the reader build a view of the tuna as a frightening creature who comes out of nowhere to eat fish, is deleted in the adapted version. Without words such as "swift" "fierce," which contribute to the building of the tuna fish as scary, it does not appear to be threatening. Instead of just "swallowing" the fish in the adapted version, the tuna, in the original, does it in "one gulp," thereby re-enforcing its size. Furthermore, by including only half of the original picture in the adapted version, the tuna appears less like a large, fierce fish in swift pursuit of other fish.

As a result of these changes, the episode is less exciting and suspenseful. Furthermore, the full form of the tuna is helpful later in the original narrative when Swimmy teaches the fish to swim in that shape.

*b. Omission of Words and Pictures*

| Original Words | Adapted Words |
|---|---|
| He swam away <u>in the deep wet world</u>. He was scared, <u>lonely</u> and very sad. | He swam away. He was scared and very sad. |

| *Original Picture* | *Adapted Picture* |
|---|---|
| In a double-page spread, Swimmy is alone in a bleak world conveyed by marbled, dark green color and white space. | This picture is eliminated. |

The descriptions of Swimmy as scared, lonely, and very sad are re-enforced by the picture. The colors are limited and muted, and Swimmy is entirely alone. The original words underscore this world.

The adapted version eliminates the words "lonely" and "deep, wet world" along with the supporting picture cues. This information helps the reader in seeing that Swimmy is a character who initially is isolated from other characters.

*c. Mismatch between Wrds and Pictures*

| Original Words | Adapted Words |
|---|---|
| But the sea was full of wonderful creatures, and as he swam, <u>from marvel to marvel</u> Swimmy was happy <u>again</u>. <u>He saw a Medusa made of rainbow jelly</u>. | But the sea was full of wonderful creatures and as he swam, Swimmy was happy. |

| Original Picture | Adapted Picture |
|---|---|
| In a double-page picture, Swimmy is shown moving toward a large Medusa made of rainbow colors shaped like a jelly fish. | A half page shows part of a "forest of seaweed." |

Several observations are evident from these alterations. The notion of swimming "from marvel to marvel" is eliminated in both words and pictures. In the original, each marvel is depicted in a double-page picture with Swimmy. This enables the reader/listener to visualize the medusa, a lobster, a "strange fish pulled by an invisible thread," a "forest of seaweed, and a long eel," and to see why the narrator referred to them as marvels.

In the adapted version, the description of Swimmy is followed by a paragraph on the same page referring to a lobster, a forest of seaweed, and an eel. As noted, the picture shows part of the forest of seaweed on a half page. Essentially, in the adaptation, valuable picture cues necessary for the reader to build a view of each sea marvel are removed. The reader does not experience the "wonderful" sea world in which Swimmy lives.

It is evident from this discussion that the adapted version of *Swimmy* changes the original in significant ways. By altering the cues Lionni selected and arranged to guide the reader in constructing the story, the adaptor created a new set of guides that more than likely will affect how the reader constructs and enjoys the story.

### Chapter 1 of *Homesick* and Its Adapted Version

The original chapter 1 of *Homesick* (Fritz, 1982) was previously used to illustrate narrative elements of character, time, and narrator. This chapter appeared as the single excerpt from the novel in a basal reader (Fritz, 1987). The first part of the original chapter included a number of references to Jean's character and to her life in Hankow, China, before the revolution. For example, information is provided about the lowly position to which the Chinese were relegated in their own culture, various Chinese customs, the foreign sections of the town, the block where the beggars sat, the American gunboats, and Jean's house with shards of glass on the wall used for protection. In the adapted version, many of these descriptions were eliminated, including those of Jean's house, her *amah* (i.e., nanny), the foreign sections of town, the block where the beggars sat, and the American gunboats. The following is the information about Jean's *amah* in the original version that was deleted in the adaptation.

> She was different from other amahs. She did not even come
> from the servant class, although this was a secret we had to
> keep from the other servants who would have made her life mis-
> erable, had they known. She had run away from her husband
> when he had taken a second wife. She would always have been
> Wife Number One and the Boss no matter how many wives he
> had but she would rather be no wife than head of a string of
> wives. She was modern. She might look old-fashioned, for her
> feet had been bound up tight when she was a little girl so that
> they would stay small, and now, like many Chinese women, she
> walked around on little stubs stuffed into tiny cloth shoes. Lin
> Nai-Nai's were embroidered with butterflies. Still, she believed
> in true love and one wife for one husband. (p. 7)

This information pertains to the status of *amahs* in prerevolutionary China, including marriage customs, feet binding, and expectations that amahs come from the servant class. Moreover, we learn that this amah broke from custom by running away from her husband and by working at a servant-class job. This information is important later in the novel when we learn that Lin Nai-Nai's family is attacked because of rising tensions among the classes. We also learn about her personality. One interpretation is that she is brave, principled, and good-natured.

Additionally, in the full-page picture of the *amah*, one of the few illustrations in the book, she is shown in traditional dress, hair pulled back, feet bound, and seated in a bamboo chair. In the adapted illustration, she is seated with Jean, and both are embroidering. Jean and Lin Nai-Nai are almost indistinguishable in their modern clothes and hairstyles. Therefore, two girls appear to be in the picture. In the original, the picture elaborates the words, whereas in the adaptation, both the descriptive words and the picture information are missing, thereby removing cultural and historical information.

Other alterations reflect omission of the narrator's assessment of her situation, including views that are critical of her teacher:

> Miss Williams was pinch-faced and bossy. Sometimes I won-
> dered what had ever made her come to China. "Maybe to catch
> a husband," mother said. A husband! Miss Williams! (p.11)

Another type of deletion provided information about Jean's personality: "Sometimes I had to stay in for talking class and write 'I will not talk in class fifty times'" (pp. 25–26). Jean describes how she did that by writing the words in columns: "So I never had to think what I was writing. It wasn't as if I were making a promise" (p. 26).

In formulating Jean's character, this response could be interpreted as indicative of her rebelliousness, along with her refusal to sing the British national anthem, noted earlier in this chapter. Therefore, the pairing of events shows how she breaks the teacher's rules and implies how she plans to continue to behave in this way.

Some of the narrator's views about being an American and thoughts about her goals also are omitted in the adaptation, as reflected in the following passage:

> For instance. I could never be president of the United States. I didn't want to be president; I wanted to be a writer. Still, why should there be a law saying that only a person born in the United States could be president? (p.10)

The theme of the narrator wanting to be a writer appears throughout the novel, but in this passage, the reader first learns about it. Readers who are aware that Jean Fritz is an author of children's books can make an intertextual link between the child character in *Homesick* and the adult author of historical fiction and biography, Jean Fritz.

## BRIDGING THEORY INTO PRACTICE

In this chapter, authors' cues related to character, time, and narration, which guide the reader in constructing and interpreting stories, are examined. Well-written texts in which the cues of authors and illustrators are effectively selected and ordered facilitate readers in their construction and interpretation of stories. When these textual cues are rearranged or omitted in adapted versions, the supports guiding storymaking are affected as well as the story that is created.

In addition to the authors' cues in storybook events, the person who reads the text aloud provides paralanguage cues that act as interpretive guides and support the listener in the meaning-making process by signaling, clarifying, and extending important textual cues. In reviewing the role of the authors' cues in the storymaking process, consider the texts in a particular classroom and how they might facilitate students' textual abilities.

- Consider the specific authors' texts featured in a classroom.

  What cues does the author provide readers to guide them in constructing characters? In understanding time relations? In discovering the narrator's position?

What visual cues does the illustrator offer viewers to assist them in the storymaking process?

How do word and picture cues work together as guides for the reader in constructing the narrative?

- Consider the role of the reader in the oral presentation of a text.

  How are paralanguage cues used in presenting the text?

  How does the reader signal, clarify, or elaborate on language and picture cues for the reader?

  How does the reader's oral interpretation and instructional text affect the author's text?

- Consider the origin of the texts.

  Are texts used in their original form as opposed to adapted versions, excerpts or both?

  If adapted texts are used, in what ways do they differ from the original text?

  If adapted texts are used, how might the alterations affect the readers' construction, interpretation, and enjoyment of a story?

# II

# STORYMAKING
# IN CLASSROOMS

# 3

# The Teacher As Mediator

In this chapter, the teachers' roles in story events are explored, with an emphasis on their ways of mediating authors' texts. A study of these roles reveals how teachers' rules and expectations socialize students into their roles as storymakers. Text events in three classrooms serve to illustrate how teachers mediate text for their students by signaling authors' cues and evoking readers' processes of constructing, interpreting, and signifying stories.

In chapter 2, cues in authors' texts were examined in terms of their roles in storymaking processes. In classroom situations, these texts are embedded in discourse events in which teachers and students enter into a dialogic relation with the text. A story is created in the dialogic meeting between two (or more) sources of consciousness. This perspective is consonant with the social semiotics framework for classroom discourse developed thus far. In an actual event involving an unfolding text, teacher and students enter into a dialogic relation with the author's utterance, transforming it into a narrative work.

The teacher often plays the dominant role in determining how narratives are generated. He or she chooses the texts, establishes the means by which students select texts, or uses the texts designated by others (e.g., district officials). With respect to the student reader, the teacher determines how stories will be constructed (i.e., the nature of the "reactive texts") and how students' texts will provide evidence of their constructive and interpretive abilities.

In addition, the teacher influences the making of the story during classroom events by framing and interpreting the texts and by responding to students' interpretations. The teacher thus participates in events by signaling certain texts as significant, by determining what counts as success in storymaking, and by influencing how the author's text will evolve into a story during the event.

The teacher also mediates storymaking events by socializing students into ways of participating in group processes. Rules and expectations regarding what is appropriate in "doing" group apply to listening behavior, turn-taking, and gaining the floor, among others.

## SOCIAL AND TEXTUAL MEDIATION

A primary way in which children experience stories is through encounters with adults who mediate them. When children interact with narrative texts in the home, library, religious and community settings, there often is an adult who guides the interaction. Purposes, rules, expectations, and conventions for participating in storymaking vary according to the requirements of the particular context. For example, the purpose of one event could be to construe a "message" associated with the narrative, whereas the purpose of another event could be to create a social interaction between an adult and a child.

The text can also serve as a vehicle for inducting the child into the "contracts of literacy" (Snow & Ninio, 1986). In this case, the adult may modify the author's message, thus adjusting it to her or his perception of the child's developmental level (as in the case of May in chap. 2). Whereas the adult often establishes the agenda for a narrative event, the child also functions as an active participant who sets and/or renegotiates agendas. The nature of the child's role, however, is influenced by the adult's expectations for the interaction.

The classroom is a community in which rules and expectations regarding storymaking exist. They are communicative settings in which not only texts, but also text events are constructed through interactions between teachers and students (Green & Wallat, 1981; Gumperz, 1986). In this context, students' texts are subject to mediation by the teacher and by other students. Students may encounter challenges to their interpretations and to their ways of participating in storymaking processes during classroom events. This can result from differences between the students' expectations regarding narrative experiences and those operating in the classroom. Such differences create problems when there is no space for negotiating alternative ways of meaning making (Heath, 1983).

Storymaking in classrooms involves establishing a discourse that reflects expectations for social and academic participation. The teacher's cues guide the students in "reading" the unfolding co-occurring verbal messages, nonverbal actions, and contextualization cues operating in the event (Green & Smith, 1983). Students thus actively participate in constructing both the teacher's expectations and the narrative work.

Teachers create the "conditions" for storymaking events by establishing rules for participation in group processes. These rules are explicit and/or implicit and communicated verbally and/or nonverbally. Expectations for "doing" group pertain to being attentive, taking turns, sitting appropriately, staying in one's space, and so forth. Rules and expectations for participation (e.g., turn-taking) suggest "ideological assumptions about the social identities of and social relationships between teachers and students" (Fairclough, 1992, p. 89).

Students actively participate in events by "reading" and reacting to the teacher's expectations for participation. Students' reactions to the social demands of the event and, in turn, the teacher's reactions to the students influence the course of the event as well as the story that is constructed. For example, when more attention is given to social management, less attention is available for interpretive processes.

In mediating text, teachers signal the author's language cues and the illustrator's visual cues as well as information pertaining to characters, time, narration, and other narrative elements through their ways of reading and talking about the text. What is emphasized reflects, in part, the teacher's knowledge of textual cues, the nature of the cues in the text and the goals of the curriculum. The teacher's questions and comments evoke students' processes of constructing, interpreting, and signifying texts. Teachers may emphasize certain processes over others depending on their views of meaning-making, the nature of the text in use, their awareness of students' needs, and so forth. In addition, teachers convey their expectations for participating in groups during story-reading and discussion.

In the following sections, the teacher's role as mediator during storymaking processes is highlighted by examining storybook reading events in a kindergarten classroom, comparing storybook reading events in a kindergarten and a second-grade classroom, and exploring a small group discussion in a second-grade classroom.

To facilitate the analysis, the teacher's responses are viewed in a social semiotic framework. For example, at the level of text, responses signal language and narrative information. At the level of discourse, responses refer to information about conducting discourse among participants. At the level of context, responses signal information about how to participate in storymaking events. Examples and definitions of these responses taken from a storybook event in a Kindergarten classroom involving Don Freeman's (1978) *A Pocket for Corduroy* are noted as follows:

1a. Text—responses pertaining to the language of the text: phonology, syntax, semantics (e.g., "What do you do in a Laundromat?") (defines a word)

1b. Text—responses pertaining to story information: character, time, narrator (e.g., "Now what did Lisa tell him [Corduroy] to do?")

2a. Discourse—responses pertaining to participants conducting discussion: turn-taking, talking one at a time, listening (e.g. "I like the way you put your hand up.")

2b. Discourse—responses pertaining to participants: personal experiences, knowledge, beliefs (e.g., "Have you ever seen a bear that looked like Corduroy?")

3. Context—how to participate in story events: staying in your seat, showing you are ready to listen (e.g., "Scoot around here so you can see the story.")

## A STORY EVENT IN DENISE'S
## KINDERGARTEN CLASS

The storybook event in Denise's class occurred in an urban kindergarten center with predominantly African American students. Denise, a European American, read Freeman's (1978) A Pocket for Corduroy to her students, illustrating aspects of social and textual mediation processes (Davis & Golden, 1994).

After the students were assembled on the rug and Denise was seated in a chair in front of the group, she set the conditions for participating in the event:

---

Teacher:   Curt, show me your best listening for group time. Abby, scoot around here so you can see the story. Today's story is called **A Pocket for Corduroy**. Eddie, I need you to be sitting and listening to the story now. Curt, I need you to read this ... Terence ... Dan ... **A Pocket for Corduroy** by Don Freeman.

---

Denise's expectations, both explicit and verbal, were evident when she asked specific students to comply with various rules (e.g., show your best listening, sit appropriately). Observations of the interaction suggest that students were previously introduced to the rule of good listening for group time. They demonstrated this by focusing their attention on the teacher rather than their peers, by sitting down, and by sitting in a position from which they could see the pictures. When two students did not comply, Denise called them by name to bring them in line with the group.

Another expectation for "doing" group concerned the requirement that students had to raise their hands to gain a turn to speak:

> *I like the way you put your hand up, Marie.*
> *I see when you wanted to have a turn.*
> *Ronnie, your hand is up. Would you like a turn?*

This exchange illustrates Denise's strategy of re-enforcing a rule by complimenting students who display the appropriate behavior. She praised Marie for raising her hand to indicate she wanted a turn and rewarded Ronnie with a turn because he raised his hand.

After "setting the conditions" for the event with regard to listening, sitting, and gaining access behaviors, Denise read the title of the book, *A Pocket for Corduroy* while holding up the front cover showing Corduroy wearing green overalls with what appears to be a sewn-on pocket. The reader can infer this from a spool of thread by his foot and a loosely stitched, unmatched pocket on the pants:

| | |
|---|---|
| Teacher: | *Cara, what do you think this is going to be about?* (several students talk) |
| Teacher: | *Who do you think Corduroy is?* (in a soft voice) |
| Cara: | *The bear.* |
| Teacher: | *You think it's the bear? Troy, who do you think he is?* |
| Troy: | *He has green pants on.* |
| Teacher: | *He has green pants on? Let's see what happens.* |

Answering the first question required a translation of the author's words in the title, with reference to the picture cues. Therefore, word and picture cues were interdependent, and the listener had to identify and link these cues.

Denise's second question also required students to translate information and make a connection between words and picture. The picture of a teddy bear in overalls is located beneath the title of the book. Although the words in the title do not state who Corduroy is, Cara answered that he is a bear. Denise restated Cara's answer in question form and asked Troy the same question, suggesting that other answers were possible. She repeated Troy's observation in question form: "He had green pants on?" Troy's response suggests that he identified who the character is by what he is wearing. Denise's comment regarding what will happen next oriented the students to see narrative as a series of unfolding events.

In the following segment, Denise's expectation for meaning-making focused on the concept of a laundromat. She first read the author's words:

"Late one summer afternoon, Lisa and her mother took their laundry to the laundromat."

| | |
|---|---|
| Teacher: | *What do you do in a laundromat?* |
| Students: | *Wash clothes.* |
| Teacher: | *You wash your clothes.* |
| Ronnie: | *My mom took me to a bear store.* |
| Teacher: | *She took you to a bear store? Have you ever seen a bear that looked like Corduroy? Jerry, what do you do in a laundromat?* |
| Jerry: | *You wash your clothes.* |
| Teacher: | *You wash your clothes.* |

As reflected in her repetition of the question, Denise's interest was on what you do in a laundromat. To answer the question, students could draw on life experiences and the picture information, which portrayed characters placing and removing clothes from washing machines and dryers.

After the exchange with Ronnie about a visit to a bear store, Denise asked Jerry about laundromats, confirming his answer by repeating it. Denise looked for a specific answer, appealing to students' conceptual knowledge. This is evident in her general framing of the questions (e.g., "What do you do in a laundromat?" versus "What are the characters doing in this picture?").

The following exchange represents an interweaving of fact-based questions and questions eliciting varied responses. Students were asked to anticipate what might happen when Corduroy looks for a pocket, to construct the events that did happen (e.g., Corduroy disobeyed Lisa), and to speculate about where Corduroy might find a pocket. In the text, Lisa told Corduroy to "sit right here and wait for me," which he did until he overheard her talking about a pocket and realized "I don't have a pocket." He slid off the chair. "I must find something to make a pocket out of," he said, and he began to look around.

| | |
|---|---|
| Teacher: | *Now, what do you think is going to happen?* |
| Student: | *He can't find it.* |
| Student: | *He's going into the washer.* |
| Teacher: | *Going into the washer. Now what did Lisa tell him to do, Jerry?* |
| Jerry: | *Sit in the chair.* |
| Teacher: | *Sit in the chair. Lida, was he listening to Lisa?* |
| Students: | *No.* |
| Teacher: | *Where is he going, Rick?* |
| Student: | *To find a pocket.* |

| | |
|---|---|
| Teacher: | *Where's he going, Rick?* |
| Rick: | *To find a pocket.* |
| Teacher: | *Where do you think he'd find a pocket, Dan?* |
| Student: | *On the floor.* |
| Teacher: | *Dan, where do you think he could find a pocket?* |
| Student: | *On a jacket.* |
| Dan: | *In the wash.* |
| Teacher: | *Do you think he'll find one in the wash? Well let's see where he looks.* |

Denise initiated this transaction by asking the students to speculate about what might happen, repeating one student's answer. Certain answers were expected in response to questions that pertained to the interaction between Lisa and Corduroy about where Corduroy was going. Answering these questions required translating the author's words.

In the last part of the exchange, Denise engaged her students in speculating about where Corduroy might find a pocket, emphasizing one of the student's conjectures by repeating it in question form. The phrase, "Let's find out," also evident in the first segment of section, suggested to the students that prediction is a part of the reading process and that their answers were open to verification or disconfirmation (i.e., "Let's see what happens").

In the following segment, Denise centered on the "facts" of the narrative as they pertained to the actions of Corduroy and the artist. The author's words reveal that he "was taking his wet laundry out of the basket and putting it into a dryer."

| | |
|---|---|
| Teacher: | *He [the artist] was taking his wet things and he wanted to do what?* |
| Student: | *Wash them.* |
| Student: | *Dry them.* |
| Teacher: | *They were already wet. What do you think he's going to do with them now that they're already wet, Troy?* (several students talk at once). |
| Teacher: | *He was putting all the wet things inside the dryer. Who was inside this wet stuff?* |
| Students: | *Corduroy* |
| Teacher: | *Corduroy. So where's Corduroy going now?* |
| Student: | *Washer.* |
| Student: | *Dryer.* |
| Teacher: | *He's going to go into the dryer.* |

In this segment, text talk was directed to a particular concept: What you do with wet clothes in a laundromat. Denise questioned students about this concept, emphasizing the word "wet" throughout the exchange. To answer the question, students had to translate textual information. Both the picture and the words revealed that Corduroy is in the basket. Therefore, the listener had to infer that Corduroy would go into the dryer. This prediction, however, did not hold because Corduroy fell out, and the artist decided to wash only his green pants.

As seen in the previous discussion, Denise was a key mediator in the storymaking processes in her roles of establishing social and textual expectations for storymaking, initiating students' interactions with the text, and responding to them. Her style of mediation was similar to that of the initiation–response–evaluation pattern described by Mehan (1979). Questions initiated responses that were verifiable by reference to the pictures and/or words, or that invited speculation about narrative elements, particularly events.

Denise confirmed "correct" responses by repeating them. Responses to speculative questions were repetitions of the students' answers or restatements of the students' responses in question form. Denise solicited, but did not probe students' responses to questions. To end some exchanges and transition into others, she remarked, "Let's see what happens."

Implicit in the storybook reading event discussed here is the notion that narrative is an unfolding of events that progresses in linear form. Denise oriented students to look ahead to events and backward in one case.

Because context is created as each event unfolds, meaning is situation specific. In approaching the same text, teacher and student participants may emphasize different aspects of the narrative and offer different responses to open-ended questions. Even though some of the facts of the text remain stable across events (e.g., Corduroy is a toy bear), the particular facts that are signaled might vary, some receiving more emphasis than others. In addition, nonfactual questions, such as prediction questions, can generate different meanings across events. The success of a storymaking event depends on a shared understanding of both the social and academic expectations operating in the event. Building shared understandings involves connecting intrapersonal factors, such as personal experiences, knowledge, and theory of the world, and interpersonal factors, such as expectations for social and academic participation in storymaking events.

Observations of Denise's class as well as interviews with her revealed that she structured storybook reading events according to mainstream expectations reflecting teacher initiated talk, student answers, and teacher responses to these answers (Davis & Golden 1994). Moreover, her rules and expectations for participation in group were indicative of mainstream values. If students' language and social behavior did not match school expectations, Denise attributed this to "environmental deficiency," and the students were referred for special testing.

## STORY EVENTS IN LENA'S KINDERGARTEN AND ANNYCE'S SECOND-GRADE CLASSES

Lena, an African American kindergarten teacher and a colleague of Denise's, and Annyce, a second-grade European American teacher, engaged their students in storybook events involving Maurice Sendak's (1963) *Where the Wild Things Are*. Annyce was an English as a second language (ESL) teacher in a reservation school in which all students were Native American (Golden & Gerber, 1990).

A comparative analysis of these two events helps to bring into focus not only the teachers' mediatory role, but also the connections between text and discourse that influence storymaking. Contrasting events enables us to speculate whether differences occurred as a result of the teachers' implicit purposes in reading, the students' roles in the event, or how the teachers scaffolded the text. Differences in patterns can be attributed to the goals of the teacher, the grade level of the students, the students' prior experiences with the text, and the contextual features of the event. Storytime in the kindergarten and a literature lesson in the second grade are contrasted in the following sections.

### Introducing the Event

Lena introduced the event by announcing that the students would hear *Where the Wild Things Are*:

---

| | |
|---|---|
| Teacher: | *Okay, we're going to hear story while you're eating—**Where the Wild Things Are. Where the Wild Things Are**. And I'm going to have Sela get our little guy out of the bucket. Our wild thing out of the bucket. He's such a wild guy. Thank you. Here's the wild guy.* (Students laugh). |
| Teacher: | *Isn't he wild looking?* |
| Students: | *Yeah* (Students laugh). |
| Teacher: | *Furry guy with red-orange hair. And a big what color nose?* |
| Students: | *Pink.* |
| Teacher: | *Pink nose. Bright yellow eyes. I'm going to sit him here while we're going to hear about this wild guy. Okay, the story is called **Where the Wild Things Are** and the person who wrote the story—the author—is called—let's see who the author is. Maurice Sendak.* |

> *He was very good. He got a chance to write the story and he was the one drawing the pictures in here, so he's very good at both....*
> *Okay, so it says* **Where the Wild Things Are,** *and this is the little boy that's going to tell you about the wild things.*

Lena asked Sela to get a stuffed animal version of a "wild thing" out of the bucket. She held it up, calling it "our wild guy." Participants talked about its appearance. This reference to the "wild guy" and Lena's comment suggests that the students had heard the story before.

Lena introduced the book by reading the name of the author-illustrator and making a positive evaluative statement about him. She stated that a little boy (versus a "narrator") would be telling the story. Specific goals for reading the story were not explicitly stated.

In contrast to Lena's introduction, Annyce explicitly stated several purposes for the event.

| | |
|---|---|
| Teacher: | *Since we have been reading about so many different fairy tale characters, we're going to do something a little different. We're going to look at some new kind of characters that are in other kinds of books, and we're going to be reading stories about those characters to find the adventures that they would have and the kinds of personalities that they may be having—that they may have. So we're going to start off with a book that a lot of you are probably familiar with called ...* |
| Students: | **Where the Wild Things Are.** |
| Teacher: | **Where the Wild Things Are,** *and it's written and illustrated by Maurice Sendak.* |
| Student: | (inaudible) |
| Teacher: | *What does it mean that it was written and illustrated?* |
| Student: | *Who wrote the book and who did the pictures.* |
| Teacher: | *Exactly.* |
| Student: | *I like to read that.* |
| Teacher: | *Great. Well the person who wrote this is illustrating it also. So we're going to get a chance to see how the person wrote the story and how he chose to illustrate his book. So what we're going to do is to take an adventure, so make sure you're in a nice comfortable place because our adventure is about to begin. Okay, here we go into adventure land. While you're listening to the story, see what kind of picture is painted in your head and see—and see maybe where* |

| | |
|---|---|
| | *those pictures are coming from. Is it coming from your mind? Is it coming from your—somewhere in the book to help you?* |
| Student: | Somewhere. |
| Teacher: | *You decide afterwards where you think it may have come from. So we're entering* **Where the Wild Things Are**, *written and illustrated by Maurice Sendak. And this got a special award. It was the Caldecott Medal. And that means that every year there's a book that's picked as a children's book, and this book happened to be picked one year as the best book. And I thought that this had a medal on it.* |
| Student: | *It doesn't have the medal on it.* |
| Teacher: | *Maybe the hardback. It was picked as one of the best picture books of the year.* |
| Student: | *How come it doesn't have your name on it?* |
| Teacher: | *We were fortunate to get all of these books. People lent us their books. And we got enough for everyone to have a partner and to share a book.* |
| Student: | (inaudible) |
| Student: | *What's that for? Does it have a dedication?* |
| Teacher: | *Oh, does this have a dedication in here? Well, I don't know if it has or not. We'll have to find out.* **Where the Wild Things Are.** *Story and pictures by Maurice Sendak. It does not have a dedication.* |
| Student: | *What's a dedication?* |
| Teacher: | *Who can tell us what a dedication is?* |
| Student: | *Who the book is for.* |
| Teacher: | *Okay, who it's for.* |

In contrast to Lena's brief introduction, Annyce had several themes in her opening phase, some of which were generated by students. One theme was her link between the previous genre, folk literature, and the present genre, modern picture storybooks, in terms of the characters' personalities and adventures. A goal of her literacy program was to develop students' understandings of narrative genres and elements (Golden & Gerber, 1990). After noting that the children were probably familiar with the book, Annyce asked about the author-illustrator. One student answered, while a second student commented, "I like to read that."

In the subsequent part of the exchange, Annyce oriented the students to the experience in several ways: (a) They would be participating in an adventure; (b) they would be finding out how the author-illustrator did his work;

and (c) they would be thinking about whether information in the book is provided by the words or pictures.

After the orientation, Annyce returned to the introduction of the picture book, noting that it had won a medal and explaining what the medal means. Students were actively engaged in this introduction, as signaled by their questions of why the medal is not on the book, why Annyce's name is not on it, and whether there is a dedication. A brief discussion of dedications followed when one student responded to another's question about what a dedication is.

## The Unfolding Event

To analyze the picture storybook events, columns are depicted in association with the episode in which they occurred (with the exception of the opening phase, which occurred before the reading-aloud process): Column 1 captures the discourse of Lena and her students and Column 2 reflects the discourse of Annyce and her students.

---

*Episode 1:* Max makes a lot of mischief and is sent to his room by his mother.

| Lena | Annyce |
|---|---|
| Teacher: *Oh boy, he had his wolf suit so he was going to make mischief—that means he's going to be kind of bad that night— and he's going to be showing off—doing something bad.* | Student: *Of a kind.* |
| *There it goes. He's— what is he doing? Chasing the dog.* | Student: (inaudible) |
| Teacher: *Chasing after the dog. He's … the up. Oh my, he's in his wolf suit and he's going to be doing all kinds of bad things.* | |

---

The participants in Lena's session began in the middle of episode 1 when she defined the word "mischief." She asked the children to identify one of

Max's mischievous actions depicted in the picture. To confirm an acceptable answer, Lena repeated the student's comments.

In this segment, Lena associated the word "mischief" with the word "bad" three times. The wolf suit also was noted with the suggestion that it is connected to the "bad" behavior. Thus, the appearance of the character was highlighted. Annyce and her students, on the other hand, did not engage in talk at this time.

| Lena | Annyce |
| --- | --- |
| Teacher: *His mother didn't like that, so she sent him to …* | |
| Student: *Bed.* | |
| Teacher: *Bed.* | |
| Teacher: *Boy, he really got it, didn't he? Do you know what happened?* | |
| Students: *No.* | |
| Teacher: *How did he look?* | |
| Students: *Real sad.* | |

When her students answered "no" in response to her question about what happened at the end of episode 1, Lena shifted to a question about Max's reaction as revealed in the illustration. Several students responded "sad." Lena repeated and extended their answer by referring back to the actions that led to Max's punishment. Annyce and her students did not engage in talk at the end of episode 1, other than two students offering inaudible comments.

*Episode 2:* Max stands in his bedroom, which turns into a forest.

| Lena | Annyce |
| --- | --- |
| Teacher: *Lots of trees. Oh my goodness. Trees are growing in his bedroom.* | Student: (inaudible) |
| Student: *… his bedroom.* | |

Teacher: *He's tickled. Doesn't he look tickled to you?*

Student: (inaudible)

Teacher: *See how clever he was? It's camouflaged. That means it's very hard to pick out, but it's still there, like when a lot of animals do when they're running. You can't see them because they blend in where they are.*

Teacher: *Look at that. Look at that wild place—his bedroom. Would you like your bedroom to look like that?*
Students: *No.*
Teacher: *No way.*
Student: *All my toys will be gone.*
Teacher: *That's right—if your bedroom looked like that.*

Student: (inaudible)

Both teachers interjected comments in the middle of episode 2. Lena described the pictures as she showed them to the children. She drew their attention to the trees growing in Max's bedroom, substituting the word "trees" for the author's word "forest." She continued her focus on the pictures by observing that the bedroom is a wild place (reiterating the word "wild") and making a personal link with the students by asking them whether they wanted their own bedrooms to look like that. She supported the student's answer about his toys.

With a reference to the word "camouflage," and a definition for it, Annyce highlighted how the pictures hide some of the details of the forest. In her approach, she introduced a new vocabulary word that reflected a visual concept instead of repeating or defining the author's words.

*Episode 3:* Max sails away to the land of the wild things.

Lena

Annyce

Teacher: *Let me hear terrible roars.*

Students: (Students roar.)

Teacher: *Oh, that doesn't sound like very many wild things. Let me hear you.*

Students: (Students roar.)

Teacher: *Let me hear you.*

Teacher: *We have some wild things in here. Now gnash your terrible teeth ...*

Students: (Students gnash teeth.)

Teacher: *... and roll your terrible eyes.*

Students: (Students laugh.)

Student: *I don't know how.*

Teacher: *Sure you can.*

Student: *I can—look.*

Teacher: *Exercise them too. And showed their terrible claws.*

Students: (Students show claws.)

Lena did not engage her students in talk at this point. In contrast, Annyce encouraged her students to take on the role of the wild things through participation. When the author said "roar," she asked the students twice to roar loudly, commenting, "We have some wild things in here." After reading the author's words, she told them to gnash their teeth and roll their eyes. When one student said he couldn't, she replied, "Yes you can."

---

*Episode 4:* Max tames the wild things.

Lena                                                    Annyce

Teacher: *Who did that to the wild things?*

Students: *The wild things.*

Student: *His mommy.*

Teacher: *His mommy—his mommy did that—treating the animals just like his mommy treated him—without their supper.*

Annyce did not ask the students to respond at this time. Lena, however, questioned her students about an earlier event by asking them who did the same thing to Max. Several students answered "the wild things," whereas one student responded "mommy." Lena sanctioned this response by repeating it and elaborating on the implicit connection between Max and his mother.

---

*Episode 5:* Max sails home to find his supper waiting.

| Lena | Annyce |
|---|---|
| Teacher: *It was a long time.* | Teacher: *How did they show you this picture was nighttime? What did they do to it?* |
| | Student: *Darkened it.* |
| | Student: *Made it dark.* |
| | Student: ... *the shadows from the boat.* |
| | Student: (inaudible) |
| | Student: (inaudible) |
| | Teacher: *Where is the shadow of the boat?* |
| | Student: *Right there.* |
| | Student: (inaudible) |
| | Teacher: *Oh, you see Max's shadow ... and you see somewhat of a shadow around the moon.... You see a difference between this shadow? You can see exactly the shape the shadow makes, and here it's just sort of foggy sort of a mist. Kind of not very clear.* |

---

In response to this segment of text, Lena rephrased the author's language regarding the time it took for Max to return home by saying, "It was a long time." In contrast, Annyce focused the students on reading the picture clues by asking how they showed that this picture was nighttime. Several students replied that they made it dark. Annyce confirmed this observation. One student remarked on the differences in shadows: Max is clearly outlined, whereas the one around the moon is "sort of foggy." (Annyce reported the student's adjective "foggy" after the event because it was not audible on the tape.)

| Lena | Annyce |
|------|--------|
| Teacher: *Boy, there's his supper over there. How does he look Now?* | Teacher: *Still …* |
| | Student: *… hot.* |
| | Teacher: *Hot.* |
| Students: *Happy.* | Student: *Why aren't there any pictures?* |
| Teacher: *Happy.* | |
| | Teacher: *That's a good question. Does anyone have an answer?* |
| | Student: *Maybe he didn't want to—maybe that's how he wanted this book.* |
| | Students: (inaudible) |
| | Teacher: *S?* |
| | Student: (inaudible) |
| | Teacher: *S, could you say it a little bit louder?* |
| | Student: *Who was it that said the question?* |
| | Teacher: *Was it S? Okay, S, can you repeat it?* |
| | Student: *Why wasn't there a picture on the last page?* |
| | Teacher: *Oh, she asked why there wasn't a picture on the last page, and a lot of you have some really good answers as possibilities. The only way to really know is to do what?* |
| | Student: *Write to him.* |
| | Teacher: *Write him a letter and see …* |

After the reading of the end of the last episode, Lena directed her students' attention to the picture of the supper on the table and asked them to look at Max and describe him. In Annyce's class, a student initiated the discussion by asking why there was not a picture on the last page. Annyce invited her students to speculate, and several offered different reasons. She ended the exchange by asking her students how they could discover the answer. One student suggested writing to the author. The next day, Annyce created a letter-writing center for this purpose.

| Lena | Annyce |
| --- | --- |
| Teacher: *That was a good story for us* | Teacher: (discussion of extension activities [e.g., constructing |
| Students: (applaud) | the character by identifying his traits; drawing a fantasy world]) |

## Comparing the Two Events

The comparison of two teachers reading the same text emphasizes the power of social discourse in shaping the narrative. Each teacher emphasized very different aspects of the author's-illustrator's text, and the events reflected different discourse interactions among participants. As a result, the works that were produced varied.

In the event in Lena's class, several patterns were evident. She focused students' attention on the main characters' actions and reactions as revealed through the illustrations. She accepted students' responses, at times extending them. She also altered the author's words by substituting one word for another to make the text more accessible to the students (e.g., "trees" versus "forest"). In one instance, Lena asked the students to interpret a situation by linking the actions of two characters together (e.g., Max's and his mother's).

Following another pattern, Lena initiated talk about the unfolding story. If students answered, she responded to their answers by repeating and sometimes extending them. Therefore, Lena's discussion followed the initiation–response–evaluation pattern discussed earlier. She interpreted the author's messages, initiated students' responses, and evaluated responses indirectly through repetition and extension. Students were not individually recognized in a turn-taking situation, but answered as a group, unlike the procedure Denise employed.

Several patterns are evident in the event in Annyce's class. First, she invited the students to take on the role of the characters telling them to dramatize the author's words by "roaring their terrible roars." Second, she focused the students on the illustrator's techniques for achieving certain effects, such as nighttime. In contrast to the event in Lena's classroom, students in Annyce's discussion initiated talk, such as asking why the author did not put an illustration on the last page, and responses of other students were encouraged.

Annyce, then, did not serve as the authority on the narrative. From a semiotic perspective, students in Annyce's class participated in listening to, constructing, and interpreting text. She mediated this transaction between the author's words and the students' talk. To support this process, she drew students' attention to the cues in the illustrator's pictures. As a follow-up activity, students interpreted their dream/fantasy worlds through their own illustrations.

It would be erroneous, however, to claim that these events are representative of textual events in each classroom. This is evident in a brief comparison between two events involving Lena and her students, and a more extended look at Annyce and her students. Although there are similarities, for example, between Lena's storybook events involving *The Little Fireman* and *Where the Wild Things Are*, there also are important contrasts. The similarities include the initiation–response–evaluation pattern and Lena's expectation of group versus individual responses. In contrast, her focus is on character actions and reactions in *Where the Wild Things Are*, whereas her emphasis is on concepts related to fire safety in *The Little Fireman*, a link from text to world (Cochran-Smith, 1984) and to opposites (e.g., high–low). This difference suggests the contrasting purposes for the events. The book on the firemen, for example, was connected to a thematic unit on fire safety.

Similarly, Annyce's lesson on *Little Red Riding-Hood* (discussed in the following section) shared common patterns with the event involving *Where the Wild Things Are* in its emphasis on analysis of literary elements: For example, students compared two versions of the folktale and identified character traits in Sendak's text. Yet, although the events shared the general goal of literary analysis, the specific approaches varied. The explicitly stated approach to the folktale was to compare and contrast the characters and events in different versions, whereas the explicitly stated goal in the reading of Sendak's text was to think about the characters and illustrations. In this sense, aspects of the folktale event involved translating textual information, thereby resembling Lena's focus on textual information in Sendak's text. It should be noted, however, that in Annyce's class, the extension activity involved students in building a profile of Max's personality, which reflected an emphasis similar to Lena's.

Another reason why it cannot be argued that one narrative event in a classroom equals another is because the participants are involved in a range of textual processes. Lena's narrative events routinely happened as the final activity in her half-day kindergarten. These events served different functions, as noted previously in the discussion. However, on occasion, she read a story to the students as an orientation to center activities during the first part of the morning. Therefore, storybook reading in Lena's class displayed both common and divergent intercontextual links and approaches.

In Annyce's class, intercontextual and intertextual connections were directly evident in her literature study unit in which the narrative texts and related concepts were arranged in a particular order (e.g., narrative characters with few traits were introduced before more complex characters). At other times during a given week, Annyce engaged the students in narrative texts for other purposes: storytelling related to the students' culture during the storytelling season, basal reader narratives highlighting particular skills, and texts read aloud for enjoyment, among other purposes.

In the following section, an event in Annyce's class involving the construction of *The Little Red Riding Hood* tale is explored.

## A STORY EVENT IN ANNYCE'S
## SECOND-GRADE CLASS

The text that initiated the event was a retelling of *Little Red Riding Hood* (LRRH) by two students. On the previous day, the students had told an oral version of the story to the class, which Annyce transcribed for the event on the second day. Thus, one (re)constructed text was matched against a second (re)constructed text. The first text, however, functioned as a primary author's text, thereby creating a semiotic chain of reactive texts. Annyce initiated the first phase of the event by informing the students about the instructional task:

> And what we're going to do is that we're going to read this together, and then we're going to make a chart to find out what we learned from this because they had a really interesting story.... Let's read the story aloud together, and then we'll look at it to find some more information about it....

After the students had read the story in unison, Annyce referred to a chart on which students would list the characters and events in the retelling. As the students identified LRRH, the grandmother, and the wolf as the characters, Annyce wrote the names on a chart under the label "characters."

Annyce then shifted the focus to the column labeled "events." "Okay, so now. What were the events of the story? What happened in the story?" Her emphasis in the discussion was not only on the events, but also on the order in which they occurred. Annyce wrote down students' responses on the chart. A segment from this discussion follows:

| | |
|---|---|
| Teacher: | *Then what happened?* |
| Student: | *He tried to sound like grandma.* |
| Teacher: | *Okay, the wolf tried to sound like Grandma.* (writes it down) *Then what happened?* |
| Student: | *Then he fell.* |
| Teacher: | *Who fell?* |
| Student: | *Grandma.* |
| Teacher: | *Grandma fell?* |
| Student: | *No.* |
| Student: | *LRRH fell.* |
| Teacher: | *LRRH fell?* |
| Student: | *She fell for it.* |
| Teacher: | *Oh, she fell for it. She fell for what? Did she fall back down?* |
| Student: | *No, she fell for the voice of grandma—for the voice of the wolf.* |
| Teacher: | *LRRH fell for the wolf's voice of grandma.* (writes it down) *So she didn't know it was a trick, did she? That she was playing a trick on her ...* |

The first question was phrased to elicit the sequential order of events: Annyce confirmed a student's answer by stating "okay," and by writing it on the chart. In the next part of the exchange, Annyce probed students about who fell and restated a student's response in question form? She apparently interpreted the student's response as meaning that LRRH literally fell down. The student, on the other hand, meant that LRRH was fooled by the voice. Using the student's language, she wrote down the response and extended it with a comment.

In the next phase of the event, students were asked to identify the characters and events in a picture book version of LRRH (Grimm & Grimm, 1971). Annyce introduced the topic in the following way:

| | |
|---|---|
| Teacher: | *We heard Jay's and Robert's version, and we looked at what was important from their story. And now what we're going to do is we're going to read a story about LRRH, and it was retold by the Lucky Book Club, and it was by Jacob and Wilhelm Grimm.... What we* |

> need to do is we need to look at this book, and as we're listening to
> this book, I want you to be thinking about how this is different than
> the version Jay and Robert wrote and how it's the same.

The same process of noting the characters and events in sequence in the
book version occurred when Annyce wrote students' responses on the
chart. In recreating the events, the students as well as Annyce monitored
the observations that other students contributed. In one part of the discussion, students disagreed on a detail and Annyce guided them toward solving
the dispute:

| | |
|---|---|
| Student: | *The wolf tried to walk.* |
| Teacher: | *And that was the end?* |
| Student: | *And then that was the end of the old wicked wolf. He fell and he died.* |
| Student: | *The stones were too heavy and he couldn't walk and he just fell down and died.* |
| Student: | *So, he only took two steps and then he fell down and died.* |
| Student: | *Three steps.* |
| Student: | *Two.* |
| Student: | *Three.* |
| Student: | *Remember one step and then he took two steps, three steps.* |
| Student: | *And then he fell down. So see, it was two steps.* |
| Student: | *Three.* |
| Student: | *Two.* |
| Teacher: | *Well, you know—you are thinking it's a little different. Is it some-thing we need to find a solution to? Do we need to find the answer to that?* |
| Student: | *No.* |
| Teacher: | *Or should everybody just have the answer that they think they want?* |
| Student: | *The answer to that, the answer to that.* |
| Teacher: | *So if we need to find the answer, where are we going to find out?* |
| Student: | *The book.* |
| Teacher: | *Okay, Jean's going to go and see if she can find out how it ended and compare it to how it was, okay? Can you read that for us? (Jean reads passage)* |
| Teacher: | *Okay, so what did she say?* |
| Student: | *Two steps and then he died.* |
| Student: | *One step.* |

| Teacher: | *He took one step, then two steps. So how many did he take?* |
|---|---|
| Student: | *Three.* |
| Teacher: | *And then he died. So how did it end? The wolf tried to walk.* |
| Students: | *He took two steps and then he fell down and died.* |
| Teacher: | *Okay …* |

In response to the students' disagreement over how many steps the wolf took, Annyce, recognizing that the students had different viewpoints, asked them whether a "solution" was needed. When a student replied that the answer was needed and Annyce asked where they should check, a student answered, "the book."

Annyce's approach was to provide a framework that actively engaged students in decision making regarding story construction and interpretation. In this way, she shared the role of mediator with the students. After students listened to the relevant words from the author, they interpreted them as saying "two steps." Annyce accepted their interpretation over the author's actual words (three steps) and most likely her own. Therefore, students served as the textual authorities on this item.

The final phase of the event focused on the comparison between events and characters in the two versions. Annyce introduced it in the following manner:

| Teacher: | *Okay now. Look what we have here. The story that was told by two of our favorite people—Jay and Robert—and we have a story that was written in a book. What we need to do is to see what's the same, and if you want to, you can look at the chart to help us figure that out. Otherwise you could use your um …* |
|---|---|
| Student: | *Mo.* (Native word for head) |
| Teacher: | *Right—memory to try to remind yourself. How are they the same?* |
| Student: | *The grandma and the mother.* |
| Teacher: | *How about if we star. I'm going to give one paper. Who would like to have one paper? Okay, Jean's going to star everything that's the same, and then I'll star everything that's the same on this one, so we'll know that they're both the same. You said that who was the same?* |
| Student: | *Grandma.* |
| Teacher: | *Okay, do you have a grandma in yours?* |

The story was perceived as having characters and events told by different narrators. Neither version was established as an authority text, but rather as a version of LRRH. The stories were essentially constructed by identifying and translating information in the author's text. Students observed commonalities in the major events and characters. It was not known whether the version the students originally heard was from Bernadette's (1971) book.

In the closing phase of the event, students were asked to draw or write about a character from the story and tell why they liked or did not like the character. After this activity, Annyce stated: "The other two groups have no idea what we did. We need to share with them." In the sharing process, the versions constituted a family of texts labeled LRRH, but they also reflected unique characteristics, thereby functioning as other texts for participants to interpret and compare.

Annyce played a major role in the evolution of the story in several ways. First, she structured the tasks and arranged them in a sequence to allow the author's work to unfold in a dynamic way. Second, she enabled the children to see that different reactive texts can be related to the same work. Third, she valued the students' text as a legitimate equivalent of LRRH that could spawn other students' constructive and interpretive activities. Finally, she followed a pattern of eliciting students' comments, writing them down, asking them for clarification, extending their responses, and rereading their observations at the end of the lesson.

## BRIDGING THEORY INTO PRACTICE

This chapter explores the important role of the discourse in which the text is embedded, with particular emphasis on the teacher as a mediator of the text and the discourse. The teacher structures the relationship among the participants, establishing the rules and expectations for storymaking. The teacher also guides the construction of the narrative, that is, the transformation of author's cues into characters, time relations, and narrators, which are integrated into the story world. In addition, the teacher may influence how the narrative will signify for students. In structuring the interaction, he or she orients students to the narrative text and how it will be read in the opening phase of the event. During the unfolding event, the teacher uses language in a variety of ways to signal aspects of the text and to make meaning through confirming, negating, and extending students' responses and through questioning.

By inquiring into the role of the teacher in mediating authors' texts for students, observe how a teacher in a particular classroom guides the storymaking process for his or her students.

- Consider how the text event is structured.

  What is the goal of the event?
  What are the rules and expectations for the event?
  How does the teacher orient the students to the event?

- Consider the roles of the participants.

  What is the nature of the teacher's talk?
  What is the nature of the students' talk?
  Is meaning socially negotiated?

- Consider the role of the author's text.

  What aspects of the author's text does the teacher signal?
  How does the teacher want the students to interact with the text?

# 4

# Constructing Reactive
# Texts in Discussion Groups

In this chapter, the focus is on the story that is interpreted by participants during group discussion. In constructing and interpreting a story after the reading process, participants in a social situation create a collective text. This story reflects individual and/or group voices depending on the participant, the goal of the event, and the features of the text. Reactive texts produced in small group discussions of fifth graders, seventh graders, and eighth graders serve as illustrations of the social construction of meaning.

In chapter 3, the discourse surrounding the unfolding text during storymaking was explored, with emphasis on the role of the teacher in mediating the text. The analyses showed that a dialogic relationship existed between the author's words and the discourse among participants, which influenced how the story was constructed and interpreted. Moreover, as the analysis of the two events involving *Where the Wild Things Are* demonstrated, the same text read in different contexts generated different emphases.

In examining the relationship between the author's text and the readers' texts, Bakhtin (1986) noted the "special kind of dialogue" between the work (the object of study) and the created, framing text (questioning, refuting, etc.) in which the interpreter's understanding takes place. In Bakhtin's view, the ready-made text and the reactive text reflect the meeting place of two subjects and two authors. Thus, the event of a text life always develops on the boundary between two or more sources of consciousness.

Teachers and students, as well as critics, create reactive texts in response to an author's text. These texts appear in different modes, including group discussions, journal responses, essays, dramatizations and so forth. Whereas some would argue that the process of interpretation is complete when the student has produced and verbalized an interpretive text (Scholes, 1982), a more compelling view regards interpretation as an ongoing, dynamic process within and across readers. Therefore, interpretation is never complete.

A major source of reactive texts is that of literary critics who produce these secondary texts that are evaluative or interpretive of the primary work (Scholes, 1982). In producing these texts, critics engage in an "institutional practice at a given time within a specific society of an accredited group of practitioners working in agreed upon ways with a recognized body of texts which constitute literature" (Hodge, 1990, p. 12). Critics observe the sociolinguistic, cultural, and literary conventions pertaining to interpretive processes in a given community. In some classrooms, the texts produced by critics function as the sanctioned interpretations of the author's text. Students in these situations read an author's text accompanied by a critic's text, which can function as the correct interpretation.

To construct reactive texts for narratives, readers apply textual strategies to produce and negotiate meaning. Engaging in the process of storymaking involves constructing the time relations of events, the characters, and the narrator(s), as noted in chapter 2. The application of textual strategies is governed by social semiotic and narrative conventions.

In the following sections, small group discussions of authors' texts in three classrooms are studied in order to explore how the author's text and participants' discourse contribute to the construction and interpretation of stories.

## ELAINE'S FIFTH-GRADE CLASS

As illustrated in the example of A Mild Attack of Locusts in chapter 1, it is useful to analyze students' discussions to discern how they construct various narrative elements and personalize the text. We can learn how students construct and interpret character traits, motivations, and changes as well as events. Discussions also enable the observer to determine how an author's text can generate similar and different constructions and interpretations. In discussions, students' interpretations may be confirmed, challenged, elaborated, or amended as a result of the social interaction. Thus, insights into both the private and public construction of texts are revealed. Limitations of this mode, however, are also apparent because some individuals talk more than others. In this section, a fifth-graders' discussion of Marguerite Henry's

(1948) novel, *King of the Wind*, is examined to explore how students construct, interpret, and signify the story.

The text relates the story of Godolphin Arabian (Sham), the forefather of the racing champion, Man O'War, and the boy who watched over him. More specifically, the first chapter of the novel, set in the present, focuses on Man O'War's last race. The narrator reports that Man O'War's owner, Mr. Riddle, liked to tell the story of his horse's ancestor, Sham. The remaining chapters convey Mr. Riddle's account of the events in Sham's life from his birth to his death, including the good and bad experiences with his various owners and his boy companion, Agba.

The five students who discussed the novel were in a reading class in a suburban middle school (Golden & Handloff, 1993). Before this peer group discussion, these students had individually read the novel and written journal entries in response to it. They were asked to discuss the novel without any other directives from the teacher. The partnership between the reader's text and the author's text is illustrated in three segments of the discussion in which students shared their perceptions of the narrator, characters, and events.

In the following segments, the students focused on how the first chapter was written. The exchange is initiated by Anne's observation that the author could have changed events.

---

| | |
|---|---|
| Anne: | *I thought they should have had the owner of ... um ... Man O'War at his house with some of his friends trying to persuade him to keep Man O' War with him.* |
| Sara: | *Yeah, and like have a conversation with him.* |
| Rick: | *Yeah, but I didn't really think that the introduction really fit in with the rest of the story.* |
| Joel: | *Yeah.* |
| Rick: | *Too much. First they're talking about the one son and he goes ...,
and then they start talking about this other retired horse.* |
| Sara: | *I know but in the last few—at the last paragraph of the introduction it said, "So I'll just have to tell you the story about King of the Wind," and then the rest of it is him telling the story about ... um ... Sham.* |
| Anne: | *I thought it was neat how when Sham was dead they didn't have an inscription on the stone and they carved it in.* |
| Sara: | *Yeah.* |
| Anne: | *And now the winds of time are erasing it like the ...* |
| Sara: | *Right. I liked the ... um ...* |

Joel:      *Some of the words I didn't understand ..., but there's like three*
           *words.*

Rick:      *Uh, oh, here it is. Here's what we were talking about. It says right*
           *here—it says in italics:*
           "And then Mr. Riddle began to think about the
           Godolphin Arabian. He had not raced at Newmarket ei-
           ther."

Anne commented that the author should have included a particular
scene between the owner of Man O'War and his friends, and Sara added
that a conversation would have been useful. Rick agreed, but indicated that
the introduction did not "really fit" with the rest of the story because it
switched from one horse to another. Whereas Joel and Sara concurred with
this observation, Sara noted that the focus on Sham was evident in the last
paragraph.

Anne switched the focus from the introductory chapter to the last chapter when she commented on Sham's gravestone, referring to how "time"
erased the inscription. During this time, Rick leafed through the book, and
after Joel's comment about the difficult words, he referred back to an earlier
part of the discussion: "Here's what we were talking about. It says right
here—it says in italics ... "

This segment illustrates how the text played an active role in the construction of the narrative, and that the students had a meta-cognitive
awareness of narrative. In the first part of the discussion, the students
showed this awareness of narrative elements not only in their formulation of
the events and the narrator, but also in their suggestion of alternative events
and their assessment of how the narrator presented the events. In addition,
Joel, Rick, and Anne referred directly to the language of the text in varying
degrees, indicating how the text itself either contributed to or inhibited understanding.

The second segment illustrates how the students were guided by the textual cues to construct their own interpretations of theme:

Sara:      *And ... um ... I liked how the wheat ear and the white spot against*
           *each other. That's like what the whole story was based on, really.*
Anne:      *Yeah, the wheat ear against the white spot.*
Joel:      *So uh ...*
Rick:      *Yeah, so it was always trying to figure out the wheat ear out. It*
           *seemed like during the middle it was taking over the white spot*
           *cause they had like ...*

| | |
|---|---|
| Sara: | *It was like ... uh ... I put in one of my journal entries it was like a former like an introduction to* **Black Beauty** *because that's almost exactly what* **Black Beauty**'s *about. Um ... that's what I like in horse stories like how they're treated badly and then something happens to them.* |
| Anne: | *Yeah.* |
| Sara: | *...* |
| Anne: | *They have the same symbols, too.* |
| Sara: | *Right.* |
| Joel: | *I thought that when ... um ... what's his face—Agba—or something that he found the white spot and the other thing on his ear.* |
| Mary: | *...* |
| Joel: | *Yeah, I thought the horse was just being ... cause it was good and it was bad.* |
| Sara: | *Yea, good against bad equals.* |

The narrator mentions the good luck symbol of the white spot and the bad luck symbol of the wheat ear when Sham is born and at several other points in the story to reflect whether the good luck or bad luck is dominant in his life. The narrator, however, does not explicitly state that the story is based on these symbols.

Sara determined that the story was based on "the wheat ear and the white spot against each other." Rick observed that the wheat ear, or bad luck, was dominant in the middle, revealing his construction of events. Sara referred to her journal entry in which she had noted an intertextual relation between *King of the Wind* and *Black Beauty*: "That's what I like in horse stories—like how they're treated badly and then something happens to them." Anne concurred and noted that the stories share the same symbols. The students, then, identified a textual reference that signaled the nature of events in the character's life.

References to the author's text also are evident in a third segment of the discussion, which focused on the construction of a character and an event.

| | |
|---|---|
| Rick: | *I wondered about Mrs. Williams, the one who had ...* |
| Sara: | *Oh, at the end.* |
| Rick: | *Yeah, they kept Sham, but they got rid of him because they couldn't stand him.* |
| Joel: | *Well.* |
| Rick: | (inaudible) |

Sara:      *You know how they went to the Boy King's palace at Ver-*
           *sailles—you know when they went there? Well, after they traveled*
           *all that way and he said something like "Why do you bring this bony*
           *horse for a present or something?" Well I mean, what do you expect*
           *from a horse that's like come all that far way.*

Sara:      *I know.*

Mary:      *He hasn't had too much food to eat.*

Sara:      *I know because they stuffed this stupid pouch that was supposed to*
           *have all this money and it was strong. I wouldn't trust that ...*

Rick:      *It says something like here—like in the beginning when we were*
           *talking about earlier it says that—in the chapter at the sign of the*
           *Red Lion:* "Agba could have been happy at the Red Lion if
           there had been only Mr. Williams."

Sara:      *Right.*

Rick:      *And later on it said:* It was Mistress Williams who made life
           hard. She was an enormous woman who went into hys-
           terics every time she saw Agba. "Mr. Williams!" she would
           shriek at the top of her lungs. "That that var-
           mint-in-a-hood! Get 'im outa of here!" *It kind of like makes you*
           *wonder like what was the problem. Like she had something bad about*
           *Agba or something. Like every time he ... she'd do, "Mr. Williams."*

Rick commented on the character, Mrs. Williams, and looked through
the book to find the reference to her role. Sara introduced a different incident that occurred when Sham was first brought to France, paraphrasing a
response from one of the characters in the French court and reacting to it.
Mary and Sara developed this view with reference to specific events in the
text. Rick referred to his earlier observation about Mrs. Williams and read
two excerpts from the text to construct this character. These examples show
how readers draw on the author's information to formulate their constructions of events and characters.

## DONNA'S SEVENTH-GRADE CLASS

In Donna's seventh-grade classes (described in chap. 1), students assumed
roles in literature circles to discuss Walter Dean Myers' (1988) novel, *Scorpions* (Golden & Canan, 1998). *Scorpions,* as noted in chapter 1, relates the
tale of a boy living in a poor urban neighborhood who struggles with deci-
sions of whether to take his brother's place in a gang, whether to keep and
use a gun he is given, and how to deal with a school bully, among other con-

flicts. Two of the literature circle roles required students to design questions to facilitate discussion, and to connect the story to self and the world.

In their role as discussion director, the students primarily produced factual and interpretive questions. Their factual questions were those that could be confirmed with reference to the text, such as "Why was Randy put in jail?" The author's text states, "Randy already knew things were going to go wrong for him because he knew he did the stickup and killed the guy" (p. 38). Other questions focused on linking messages throughout the text, such as "What did Jamal do with the gun?" Depending in part on how much of the text they had read, respondents might answer that he took the gun from Mack, pointed it at Dwayne during the fight, gave it to Tito to hide, took it to the Scorpions' hangout, asked Tito to hold it while he talked to Angel and Indian, or threw it into the dumpster.

The students' interpretive questions reflected a wider range than their factual questions. One type of question focused on a character's perceptions of another character: "Why do you think that Jamal's dad is on his back?" Another explored a character's motivation for action: "Why did Jamal join the Scorpions?" A third questioned why a character felt a certain way: "Why was Jamal's mother unhappy?"

These questions drew on a student's ability to infer, and to generate questions where more than one answer is possible in some cases. For example, to respond to the question concerning the behavior of Jamal's father, the reader could rely on the father's comments to Jamal, flashbacks to the father's role in the family, or Jamal's thoughts about his father, or go beyond the characters' viewpoints.

A fourth type of question addressed the character's personality. To answer this question, students could refer to the character's actions, speech, thoughts, and other characters' perceptions, combining these textual perspectives and moving beyond them to formulate an interpretation.

In the following segment from one discussion group, Tina's questions in the role of discussion director sparked several responses:

---

Tina:      *Do you think Jamal is a good friend? If yes, why? If no, why?*
Shannah:   *I think Jamal was a very good friend to Tito, but in a way, I don't because he was a good friend because he always listened to Tito until he told—until Tito told him to get rid of the gun and he didn't get rid of the gun because he thought that he was gonna—Dwayne was gonna beat him up, and so he kept the gun to scare Dwayne so that Dwayne can leave him alone, and so him and Dwayne did not talk about their problems, but it was still okay.*

Marv:     *I think Tito was a better friend than Jamal because Tito did something life risking—it was life risking—for Jamal, his best friend. But Jamal, he was okay because he tried—he did everything he could to try to get his brother out of jail.*

Mitch:    *Tito and Jamal, I think are—I think Jamal is a very good friend because he was very smart and good to Tito and Tito was—good back then they were both good friends.*

Tina's question about whether Jamal is a good friend invited participants to interpret and to judge Jamal's words and actions in relationship to Tito. In her response, Shannah implied that friendship is based on listening to the advice of your friend, which Jamal did not do when Tito wanted him to get rid of the gun. However, she explained Jamal's behavior as motivated by his fear of Dwayne. Marv argued that Tito is a better friend because he risked his life for Jamal by shooting the gun. He also credited Jamal for trying to help out his brother. Mitch offered a summary statement that said both Tito and Jamal are friends because they are good to each other.

Another question posed by Tina called for participants to interpret information both within and beyond the text:

Tina:     *How do you think Jamal was affected by what Tito did? Give details.*

Shannah:  *Actually, I think Jamal was shocked at Tito because Tito was always telling him to get rid of the gun, and so when Jamal was telling—told Tito to hold the gun because he didn't want no trouble between Indian and Angel, it appeared that they set him up for failure because Indian said that he was gonna be there by himself. And so Angel came out and start—and he pulled out the knife and tried to kill—and tried to kill Jamal, and so Tito was helping his friend out like he said he was.*

Mitch:    *I think Jamal was very affective because I don't think Jamal was expecting that Tito would shoot the gun. He just told him to hold it and bring it to him, so I don't think—I think he was very affected.*

In response to Tina's question, Shannah answered that Jamal was shocked at what Tito did because he told him to hold the gun, but Tito by shooting Angel and Indian saved his life. Mitch thought that Jamal was affected by it because he had not expected Tito to shoot the gun.

Whereas the primary questions asked by discussion directors were factual and interpretive, the main type of question asked by the connectors was associative. One type of associative question such as "Have you ever been asked to be in a gang?" directly addressed the reader's real-life experience in relation to Jamal's experiences. A second type asked students to place themselves in a character's position and to consider whether they would act as the character did: "If you were Jamal, would you take the gun Mack was going to give him?" To respond to a third type of question, students first had to interpret a character and then consider whether they knew someone similar: "Do you have a friend or family member like Tito?" A fourth type of question invited students to speculate about whether they might use a gun: "Would you pull out a gun on somebody?"

An excerpt from the same discussion group illustrates how Mitch, the student in the role of connector, generated a discussion among group participants:

---

Mitch: *Place yourself in Jamal's place. Would you have kept the gun? Why or why not?*

Tina: *No, I would not have kept the gun. I would have either took it to the police or threw it away somewhere. If someone catches you with …*

Shannah: *I would have kept the gun because I just would not have told no one about it and—so that I'd of kept the gun because I was a boy. If I was Jamal, I'd have kept the gun because he did not know how to fight and things like that. He didn't have no one around to help him but Tito and Tito wasn't really much of a fighter. And he needed that for protection, too.*

Alden: *… I agree with Tina because what if his mother would have found that gun? Then he would have been in deep trouble and she would of been asked—his mother would of asked what you doing with that gun, and then and then if he would of told her that he was in a gang, he would of got in more trouble.*

Marv: *I don't think that Jamal should have kept the gun because … I think that Jamal shouldn't have kept the gun because it just caused more problems in his life. I think he should went with his problem to his mom before he decided to take it into his own hands.*

Shannah: *I think that was a very good comment that Marv said and I agree with that because that's what most people say kids are asked to do anyway—do not take matters in their own hands.*

---

Several students agreed with Tina that Jamal should not have kept the gun, but for different reasons. Alden thought it would get him in trouble with his mother, whereas Marv observed that a gun can cause trouble. Shannah initially contended that Jamal should have kept the gun for protection, but later agreed with Marv that you shouldn't take matters into your own hands. It appears, then, that Shannah's opinion of Jamal's actions was influenced by another participant's views.

## MARSHA'S EIGHTH-GRADE CLASS

Five students and their teacher, Marsha, in an alternative school (described in chap. 1) participated in a small group discussion of Roald Dahl's (1974) short story, The Wish (Golden, 1986), for the purpose of making sense out of it. This group was composed of students different from those participating in the discussion of A Mild Attack of Locusts (referred to in chap. 1), although they were members of the same class. Marsha initiated the discussion by making an observation about the ending:

| | |
|---|---|
| Teacher: | *The end was very strange.* |
| Mike: | *I didn't think it's real. I just think the kid has a wild imagination.* |
| Amy: | *Yeah—he imagines everything.* |
| Paul: | *I didn't think it was real. He was building himself up like, "Oh my God, if I touch this I'm dead."* |
| Teacher: | *It was all internal?* |
| Paul: | *It must have been like the white hitting the black or something, and in his imagination he sees things moving or something.* |
| Neal: | *Or it's all in his mind that—what the pain was, you know, that he touched the black and there was pain.* |
| Teacher: | *So you think it was completely his imagination at the end there?* |
| Amy: | *Yeah.* |
| Neal: | *Yeah, he was like playing a game.* |
| Mike: | *Yeah, like he just psyched himself up—he psyched himself up so much. I'm not even sure like when he was lost in the woods he just might have been pretending that he was lost or something.* |

In this exchange, the students confirmed each other's observations that the character's imagination is the central focus of the story. Marsha asked two questions that served to clarify the students' interpretations. In the last statement, Mike referred to an earlier event that he felt illustrated the same imaginative characteristic. In the following segment, Paul and Neal apparently did not remember or link this event to support the character's imagination:

| Paul: | *Lost in the woods?* |
|---|---|
| Mike: | *... or when he was talking about ...* |
| Neal: | *Why do you say it was almost as bad as when he was lost in the woods?* |
| Teacher: | *Lost inside the woods he gets that same feeling of fear.* |
| Mike: | *When he used to walk in back on the long step-stones without touching any cracks, it sounds like the kid does this kind of thing a lot and he just really has a wild imagination.* |
| Amy: | *He just doesn't have anyone else to play with, so he does games with himself.* |
| Reed: | *It's just his way of entertaining himself.* |
| Teacher: | *He has a really vivid imagination and a vivid internal world.* |

In this transaction, Marsha answered a student's question, and Mike built on this with a specific example. Marsha's last statement summarized what the students interpreted.

In the following segment, participants continued to interpret the character's imaginative games, referring to the actions of the character. Paul built on Marsha's and other participants' comments concerning the character's imagination:

| Paul: | *Right. If he got out.... that'd be too easy.* |
|---|---|
| Neal: | *He'd be crazy.* |
| Reed: | *It was sort of like it wasn't just a carpet ...* |
| Neal: | *Like a jungle.* |
| Teacher: | *Right, and he was setting himself up a challenge.* |
| Mike: | *Like when he stepped on the yellow island, he was thinking this is an island. This is a safe spot. He wasn't just thinking it was a yellow carpet; he was thinking it was a safe spot.* |
| Neal: | *Yeah, but when he like stepped like real real close to the black, if it was like real, the snake could have just gone out and got his foot you know, he wouldn't have just stood there if it was real.* |

The discussion of the character's imaginative game-playing lead to Marsha's link between the character and herself. Her comments stimulated students' childhood memories.

| Teacher: | *This was very evocative of my childhood. I did things like that all the time. Did you feel that way about it?* |
|---|---|

Mike: *I do things like that too, you know. I'll try getting into the bathroom without touching the floor. I'll jump from one end.*

Amy: *When we walked out to recess we used to always not step on the cracks.*

Teacher: *Step on the cracks and you'll break your mother's back.*

Neal: *I remember that.*

Paul: *I used to do that when I was a kid. And if you jump you'd go "Oh" like Mike was saying if you'd jumped into the bathroom without touching the floor, right? And if you'd miss, you'd say, "Aw, man, I got 'em."*

Neal: *Well, I can remember one time when I was about three, I did step on a crack and I started crying 'cause I was afraid that I broke my mother's back.*

Teacher: *And it was that real for you.*

In a later segment of the discussion, the participants developed the idea of how real the events seemed even though they were in the character's imagination. Marsha initiated this sequence by shifting from the topic of the students' personal experiences to the author's techniques:

Teacher: *But I mean he really makes that real, really builds that up in a wonderful way.*

Reed: *It seems like it's real.*

Mike: *Yeah, when the kid starts to fall, you say, "Save yourself, save yourself," like he's going to die if he touches it. You really get that feeling.*

Neal: *Why didn't he use his hands?*

Mike: *He did—he put them on the yellow part of the carpet and pushed himself.*

Paul: *He couldn't reach any yellow—he was stretched. He didn't want to jump 'cause he didn't think he could.*

Neal: *Like a big wide black band of like red and black was underneath him.*

Reed: *For a while you think it's just a rug. Every now and then you think, well, is it real? At the end it's outside his mother's house and it makes you wonder what's he doing in there and why doesn't his mother know he's there.*

Mike: *It was like each step the kid took it was becoming more of into a like world than a rug like more into a separate area like his own imagination.*

Another link made with personal experience is evident in Marsha's statement, "I liked the part at the beginning about picking off the scab." This statement prompted a discussion on how this incident was used by the author to reveal something about the character:

| | |
|---|---|
| Reed: | *That was quite real.* |
| Paul: | *He was just sitting there picking off his scab.* |
| Neal: | *That was what built it up because he saw it laying there on the carpet, and then he realized how big the carpet really was.* |
| Teacher: | *Right.* |
| Mike: | *I think like picking up the scab kind of got him in the mood for like something deadly.* |

The participants then discussed their own experiences picking off scabs, and again, Marsha brought the experience back into the story world:

| | |
|---|---|
| Teacher: | *I think everybody has that kind of feeling, so you're immediately put right into that world—the child's world.* |
| Mike: | *It starts off with the kid's action.* |
| Reed: | *It starts off with something that you can relate to.* |
| Teacher: | *Yeah, you can really relate to it.* |
| Mike: | *It was almost as if picking off the scab was like its own separate game.* |
| Amy: | *It said it was a temptation he could never resist or something.* |
| Teacher: | *Right, yeah. And then he immediately he goes into another game, so you also have a feeling this is a child who lives.* |
| Reed: | *The scab always presented a special challenge.* |
| Teacher: | *Special challenge.* |
| Reed: | *So the rug is another challenge.* |

The discussion illustrates how Marsha used discussion strategies to evoke and respond to the students' interpretation of the text. In the discussion, she functioned as a coparticipant, yet initiated responses evoking personal experiences similar to those of the character. Instead of using only a question and answer technique, Marsha employed the strategy of making an observation such as "This was very evocative of my childhood," which stimulated the students to bring in their own experiences. In other cases, she confirmed and extended students' responses.

Another role Marsha performed involved influencing the topic of discussion such as introducing personal experience connections and then shifting to observations about the role of the author: "But I mean he [Dahl] really makes that real, really builds that up in a wonderful way."

In this internally focalized narrative, the story is revealed through one character's point of view. Events occur, or seem to occur, as a result of the character's imagination. Suspense builds as the imaginative game progresses. It is uncertain at the end whether the game is real or imaginary. It is not surprising that the discussion focuses on the character and his imagination, the lines between reality and fantasy, and the participants' recall of their own imaginative games as children. This suggests that the author's words are instrumental in guiding the reader toward similar interpretations.

This conclusion is supported by a second group's discussion of *The Wish* in Marsha's class. Again, topics focused on the character's imaginative traits, the line between reality and fantasy, and the participants' recall of their own imaginative experiences. Whereas Marsha's questions generated some of the responses, students also posed questions that were asked by Marsha in the previous discussion, particularly those pertaining to personal experiences.

In addition to the main foci of the discussions, the two group's discussions of the story differed on some topics. For example, group 1 considered the setting details, whereas group 2 commented on the style of writing and the story genre. In addition to suggesting that author's words guided the interpretation of the stories, we also could posit that similarities in interpretations occurred as a result of the participants being part of a shared interpretive community (Fish, 1980).

## BRIDGING THEORY INTO PRACTICE

In this chapter, students' processes of constructing and interpreting stories during small group discussions are explored. Guided by cues in the classroom discourse, it is possible to observe what happens in a narrative event as participants react to an author's text. The discussion illustrates how individual students express their viewpoints, which are confirmed, modified, challenged, and extended as each group builds a collective reactive text. Participants are in the position of reading the author's textual cues as well as other participants' discourse cues to construct meaning through social interaction. The outcome of the dialogic relation between the author's text and the classroom discourse is a reactive text, a text upon a text, as Scholes' (1982) said, "which itself is open to construction and interpretation."

In exploring how participants construct and interpret stories, observe group discussions of literature in a particular classroom and the nature of the reactive texts that emerge.

- Consider the role of the discussion format.

  How does the organizational structure of the group affect storymaking?
  How do the requirements of the group task influence storymaking?

- Consider the role of the author's text.

  Does the author's text affect the discussion?
  Which textual cues are brought into the discussion?

- Consider the role of the participants.

  What are individual students' contributions in storymaking?
  How are individual students' meanings affected by other students' views?
  What is the effect of the teacher's participation in the discussion?

- Consider the nature of the reactive text.

  How does the text created in the discussion relate to the author's text?
  How does the reactive text, a collective text, reflect socially constructed meanings and interpretations?

# 5

# Individual Readers' Reactive Texts

The focus of this chapter is on how individual readers transform authors' texts into stories through connecting, predicting, inferencing, and integrating information to formulate narrative elements. These processes are evident in the variety of reactive texts that students produce in classroom settings. Examining readers' reactive texts provides information about how they draw on the author's text and resources outside the text to construct and interpret stories. Examples of students' reactive texts at different grade levels illustrate their role in storymaking.

Readers do more than assemble the narrative. They also engage in interpretive activities such as weighing and valuing information and drawing conclusions about the narrative world. Moreover, the reader finds significance in the narrative by connecting it to self and world. The outcome of these and other textual practices is a story world, theoretically reflecting equal parts of the text and the reader (Iser, 1978).

In classroom contexts, the reader may be expected to voice his or her interpretation of the story world in oral, written, or visual form for the teacher, and perhaps classmates. These productions also are social in nature. Individual texts are influenced by the teacher's expectations of what kind of texts are acceptable. Because these articulations provide glimpses into stories readers create from authors' texts, the teacher reads students' responses for purposes of assessment.

## AUTHORS' TEXTS AND READERS'
## REACTIVE TEXTS

As readers read authors' texts, they construct mental representations of story worlds. Different narratives are constructed in relation to a given author's text both within and across readers. These narratives are both similar to and different from other narratives. As suggested previously, similarities can be attributed, in part, to "facts" of the text and shared interpretive conventions in a community, whereas differences can be traced to the capacity of language to generate multiple meanings, the reader's personality and sociocultural background, and the contextual expectations governing discourse practices.

Together, the narratives generated from an author's text constitute a family of texts, with each member bearing a resemblance to another (de Beaugrande, 1980). This does not, however, suggest that all constructions are equally plausible or even acceptable. It is possible, for example, for a reader to misread a word or phrase, thereby building an interpretation on an inaccuracy. Thus, a given author's words generate multiple, plausible interpretations or implausible interpretations as in the case of misreadings. There is no one constructed work, however, that merits the position of a "correct" interpretation.

Because a story is conceived as a mental representation that evolves from the reader's interaction with an author's words, the story is in the "tacit" dimension (Polanyi, 1966). Although glimpses into this text can be ascertained through the reader's voicing of that text in words or pictures, the text does not capture all that is in the tacit dimension. Furthermore, the various ways of expressing mental representations (e.g., retellings, response journals) place further limitations on what we learn about the reader's text. This suggests that multiple and diverse modes of expression provide greater access to the reader's understanding than does a single mode. Just as there is no one-to-one correspondence between an author's messages and a reader's text, so, there is no one-to-one correspondence between a reader's articulated text and his or her mental representation of a story.

## READERS' REACTIVE TEXTS
## AND STORYMAKING PROCESSES

### Mitch's Texts

By examining a reader's voiced text, we can gain insights into a range of processes in which the reader engages during interactions with a text. In their review of studies on response processes, for example, Beach and Hynds (1990) identified processes of engaging, conceiving, connecting experiences and attitudes toward literature, problem solving, explaining, interpreting, and judging. These studies employed a variety of modes for eliciting responses.

Mitch's written responses to essay questions about *Scorpions* serve as a basis for exploring processes of constructing, interpreting, and signifying text. Mitch was a participant in the small group discussion in Donna's seventh-grade classroom explored in chapter 4.

## Constructing Stories

The reader's text reveals how he or she participated in various cognitive activities associated with constructing the narrative, such as translating the author's language. The reader might express how a character performed a certain action, as is evident in Mitch's response to *Scorpions*.

> *One choice [Jamal made] was when he took the gun.*

Readers' comments also provide information about how they combined information into elements of character, time, and narrator. The reader's conclusions about a character's personality, relationships among events, or the nature of conflicts suggest that the reader has linked textual information together to form a pattern. In another response, Mitch connected several events:

> *If Jamal didn't join them [the Scorpions], then they wouldn't have the gun and Tito wouldn't have had to move away.*

Because story information is not always explicitly stated, the reader's conclusions reflect processes of inferring, translating, and linking of textual information. The reader's views of the narrative world reflect his or her connection of textual elements into a narrative. In the following example, Mitch linked the textual perspectives of character with event:

> *Jamal and Sassy were always fighting and arguing. The mother kept the relationship together because the father was never there at the hard times.*

Mitch's response illustrates the reader's role of filling in the blanks to integrate narrative elements.

## Interpreting Works

In constructing works, readers read the text, building story elements and formulating a story world. In interpreting texts, readers make meaning of story worlds. Beach and Hynds' (1990) review of studies on interpretive processes investigate readers' descriptions or conceptions of text. Such responses are similar to what Scholes (1985) denoted as creating a "text upon text" (p. 31).

Readers' texts provide insights into their interpretation as well as their construction of narrative texts. Such texts can reveal, for example, a reader's assessment of a character's motivation, whether a character is static or dynamic, and how a character's life is shaped by a particular sequence of events. Character interpretation is evident in Mitch's observation about Jamal:

> *He was so caught in fighting Dwayne, he couldn't focus on his studies. Instead of working on his work, he worked on his pride and reputation.*

Readers' responses can indicate their perspectives on central themes in a narrative as well as their views concerning the author's purpose in writing a text. Mitch contended, for example, that the author "sent a message to teenagers":

> *Don't follow in Jamal's footsteps. The footsteps were all those bad things he did. One major one was the gang. Gangs are never good. Jamal never got or wanted help. He should of gotten help from someone. Don't let your problems get bigger. What the author wanted the reader to take away from this book is what the author was saying about gangs, guns, violence, and his school problems.*

Other instances of interpretation are evident when the reader attributes meaning to significant symbols, figurative language, literary allusions, and cultural codes. In these and other ways, readers' texts are windows into their interpretations associated with narrative.

## Signifying Works

Studies that explore how readers contextualize the story consider how personal attitudes and experiences are incorporated into responses as well as connections to other texts (Beach & Hynds, 1990). Experiencing the effect of a text, however, involves not only connecting the text to self and the world, but also "transcending" self to achieve a new perspective (Iser, 1978). Readers' responses contribute information about how a reader determines the significance of a narrative by contextualizing it. For example, Mitch was critical of the choices Jamal made, and revealed his value system through prescriptive comments:

> *Along the way Jamal should have made different choices. Actually, all of his choices should have been different.... Every bad choice leads to another one. Just like when you tell a lie. Sometimes you can't stop.*

Another way that the reader contextualizes the narrative text is by establishing relationships between an author's text and other texts constructed in relation to it, that is, by establishing *intertextuality*. By considering how readers connect the narrative to things outside the story world in their responses, it is possible to learn readers' views concerning the significance of narratives.

## READERS' TEXTS IN THE CLASSROOM

Aspects of the reader's reactive texts are articulated in a variety of ways in classroom settings. In some classrooms, readers' texts are primarily revealed in their answers to the teacher's or curriculum designer's questions during or after the reading process, in answers on objective and essay examinations, and in workbook activities. In other classrooms, a wider range of modes is encouraged including journal writing, dramatic interpretation, group discussions, artistic interpretation, and free-choice writing, among others. Each of these modes provides information about the reader's text, although some may provide fewer insights than others (e.g., responses to closed-ended literal questions vs. open-ended interpretive questions). Therefore, any judgment of readers' abilities to construct, interpret, and signify narrative text should consider the nature and the limitations of the mode of expression.

The correspondence between the author's text and a reader's text is an important issue to consider with reference to classroom settings for several reasons. First, there may be an assumption that the voiced text in any form stands for the reader's construction of the author's text. Second, there may be a tendency in some classrooms to access the same aspects of the reader's text through a limited range of modes, such as answers to literal questions about the text. Third, it may be assumed that there is one correct construction and interpretation of an author's text. In some classrooms, this "correct" text is the one that coincides with the teacher's text, the critic's text, or the curriculum designer's text. Yet, whereas some aspects of story can be agreed on by a community of readers, such as the particular events that occurred and when they occurred, where the story took place, and what happened at the end, other aspects such as interpretations of character, conflict, and theme are open to multiple interpretations. Because a narrative is never fully realized (i.e., all of its possible interpretations are never captured), it can never have fixed boundaries or fixed meanings.

Which narratives are evoked in the classroom and how they are viewed in terms of acceptability reflect, in part, the teacher's theory of storymaking. By using only questions with right or wrong answers, the teacher is operating on the assumption that a text has right or wrong interpretations and that answers to certain types of questions demonstrate students' ability to construct a work. Therefore, if students construct alternative interpretations, these may be perceived as inaccurate. In this way, the teacher functions as the authority on the story. Another teacher may accept a range of interpretations in a variety of expressions if the reader is able to support his or her interpretation. This latter approach reflects a belief that there is a role for both the reader and the author's text.

An examination of the teacher's role as text authority is illustrated by his or her use and assessment of students' texts. If a limited range of interpretations is permitted, then the teacher is conveying that meaning is in the author's text. Well-informed readers such as teachers or critics create an equivalent story. If comprehension questions and retellings are the sole measure of students' texts, then the teacher is supporting the notion that a narrative text is a fact-based text that generates convergent stories. Alternatively, in a classroom where different interpretations are voiced in a variety of modes, the teacher is conveying the concept that texts generate multiple meanings that can be voiced in different ways. As Hiebert (1991) observed concerning literacy learning, "the basis for assessment is the teacher's vision of literacy" (p. 511). Concomitantly, the teacher's "vision" of narrative texts guides his or her assessment and interpretation of students' articulated texts.

In the following sections, students' texts are explored to determine what they can tell us about texts and storymaking processes. The intent is to examine the text the student produces in response to the author's text. Different modes of representation are used to illustrate how a particular mode can provide perspectives on readers' texts. Retellings and reenactments involve the students' (re)construction of the author's texts. Writing sequels and modern versions requires producing a "new" work based on a (pre)constructed text. Journal writing and peer group discussion evoke a range of responses reflecting processes of constructing, interpreting, and signifying texts.

## STUDENTS' TEXTS

### Oral Retellings

Retellings help us to understand readers' memory and organization of textual information and the story schemas they bring to the reading event. Retellings also have the potential to provide information about readers' construction of stories, although this mode of representation has not been fully tapped in this respect. Retellings, for example, can reveal readers' awareness of textual indicators of narrative elements. To illustrate this, two students' retellings of a folktale are described to show their awareness of character indicators. As discussed in chapter 2, character indicators include direct statements by the narrator; the character's speech, actions, and thoughts; and perceptions of other characters.

Children from a kindergarten–first-grade class in an inner city alternative school retold Zemach's (1965) picture book of a Russian folktale, *Salt* to a research assistant. They were participants in a study on the development of emergent textual abilities conducted by King and Rentel (1981). In the folktale, the author uses a variety of textual indicators of character. The principal indicators are the character's speech (e.g., "It was not really I that boasted but my happiness") and the character's actions (e.g., "Ivan … secretly poured the right amount of salt into all the stews and sauces"). Other indicators are direct definition by the narrator (e.g., "His elder brothers … were very jealous), appearance (e.g., "beautiful princess), other character's perceptions (e.g., "You would do nothing but sing songs to the moon"), and the character's thoughts (e.g., "Ivan realized his advantage").

*Judy's Text.*  In her retelling, Judy assumed the role of an overt, nonfocalized narrator recounting the major events in the beginning, as well as the complication and resolution of the story. Judy's retelling also reveals her awareness of a range of character indicators paralleling those used by the author. In the beginning of her retelling, Judy identified the son's father as a king (versus a merchant in the author's text) who "wanted to go somewhere on a boat," and whose father "saw how much he wanted to go."

In the complication, Judy showed the son through his action of obtaining salt: "He took a big pile of salt." By mentioning action and indirect speech, she revealed the son when he approached the king: "And he went up to the king and asked if he wanted some salt." After reporting that the king declined, Judy noted Ivan's thoughts in the following words:

*And the king's son was very disappointed and then he had an idea. He went to the kitchen and he put salt in every bowl of food that the king's helper made.*

Judy stated that after the plan succeeded, the son asked the king again to trade the salt for a specific price:

*It's two inches of gold and one inch of silver.*

Judy reported how the son "took the princess on the boat" and "met his brothers." She introduced a new character, the giant, through a description of his appearance:

*And he had a big moustache with mittens on it that were left out from the rain to dry.*

At the end of her retelling, Judy used indirect speech, similar to the author's, to reveal how the son told the father about everything that had happened:

*And he told him about the bet that the king made with him, and he told him about what he did in the kitchen and what he did with the princess.*

Judy noted how the king revealed his perceptions of his younger son's character when he referred to what the son had done in an address to his eldest son:

*You're not going to marry the princess. He is because he did all the work.*

**Stanley's Text.**    Whereas Judy's retelling focused on information throughout the story, Stanley's retelling centered on information at the beginning and in the initial part of the complication. His retelling, however, also signaled character, time, and narrator. Through direct statement by an overt, nonfocalized narrator, Stanley noted the trade of the father, appropriately substituting storekeeper for merchant, and the relationships among the family members at the beginning of his retelling:

*Once upon a time there lived this old storekeeper and he had three sons.*

Through indirect speech and direct reference to the position of characters in the family, Stanley set the stage for the initial conflict:

*And one day the storekeeper said to two of his oldest sons, "Go out and get some gold," and the littlest son said can he go with the bigger ones.*

Stanley also noted the father's perceptions of Ivan in his response to Ivan:

*And the storekeeper said "no" because he was too little and he would sing into the moon and try to make the fish dance and come back with his head cut off.*

Stanley showed Ivan's spirit when he persuades his father to let him go: "I wouldn't do that father. Would you let me go?"

Stanley portrayed Ivan through his action of making his own boat: "And he made his little self a boat out of sticks and wood and gold." Through action and direct definition Stanley initiated the complication part of tale: "And so Ivan the little boy rode off in his boat." Subsequently, Stanley referred to the character as "Ivan the dummy."

Through actions, Stanley told how Ivan obtained the salt:

*He came up to a big path leaded to a big hill on top of a great big hill [and] put all of his pieces off of his boat and threw them into the river and loaded his boat with salt.*

Through Ivan's speech and actions, Stanley reported that Ivan asked the king, "Would I have some gold for this salt?" Through action, Stanley states, "Ivan slipped into the kitchen and put salt in the food." After the king tasted the food and summoned Ivan, "it was too late and the little boy was gone and they couldn't catch him."

An analysis of Judy's and Stanley's retellings illustrate their awareness of textual indicators of character, time, and narrator. Both children showed this awareness by drawing on direct statements by the narrator, the character's direct and indirect speech, the character's actions, and other characters' perceptions. Judy also drew on the character's thoughts and appearances in her rendition.

In retelling a narrative, the student produces a text in relation to an author's text, thereby presenting a series of events in a linear sequence, with the (re)teller assuming the role of a narrator. This is evident in the (re)teller's production of various events that characters enact and react to in a designated time and space. Thus, retellings provide insights into students' awareness and use of textual indicators that guide the construction of narratives.

## Oral Reenactments

In her kindergarten classroom (discussed in chap. 3), Lena encouraged students to read books to their "friends" in the book corner during the time before formal group time and as an option during center time (Davis & Golden, 1994). These "friends" included stuffed dolls, other children, or adults.

In one such event, an adult had read Mercer Mayer's picture storybook, *What Do you Do With a Kangaroo?* to several children, and one child had asked to read the story to the adult and to other children. Textual information pertained to events in which different animal characters invaded the house of a little girl who tried to "throw them out." In the potential text, repetitive questions and responses were posed to capture the intrusion of each new character into the girl's home, such as "What would you do if a kangaroo was in your room ... ? You'd throw him out that's what you'd do. Get out of my house you kangaroo?" Each accompanying picture shows the animal creating havoc in a room and the girl trying to push or pull it out. In the end, the girl gives up and lets them all stay.

*Sanda's Text.*    Sanda read the story (although she did not decode print) in the following way:

> She was peeping behind the tree and she planted some flowers. And she said, "who's in my bed?" Then she broke off his tail when he—and she ate the boy's tail. And she saw him with a whole lot of toothbrush brushing his teeth. And he still had the toothbrush, and she pulled his tail and let him got out the door. So he stretched her pants and she said—and he said "Get off, get off." And he went downstairs and he ate the cereal where she was ready to pour it. So they looked like ... they got cabbage on the floor. And he got in—she tried to push him back but she couldn't. He said a big tiger would—a big tiger would bring ... And he said—and he said "Get off of my bike." I'm almost done. Then he eating my washcloth ... and breaking my cup. Then she pulled one and he was still eating my washcloth. How she was going to pull them all out? How she was going pull them all out? (Adult: I don't know. I wonder.) What you do if you couldn't throw them all out? (Adult: I'd let them stay.) No, he would mess up your room. Your mom would get you for that. (Adult: I don't know what I'd do.) When they was ... and they ain't listening to them. And one of them eating her hair. And one of them eating her shirt. Right? What you do if you let them tore your shirt or eat your shirt? (Adult: I don't know.) Well why? (Adult: I'd tell them not to.) So they all would sleep with her, so she thought they'd left, but they didn't.

Sanda demonstrated her concept of the story by reading left to right, and by constructing and telling the story as she looked at the pictures. At least two processes were apparent. First, Sanda told what occurred in the pictures, maintaining the notion of the character wanting to get the animals out, thereby (re)creating the interchange between characters reflected in the author's words. Second, she restated the words of the character (e.g., "Get out"), with accompanying intonation patterns similar to those of the adult reader. Moreover, Sanda paused, as the adult reader had, to invite the listener to answer the author's question: "What would you do?" In this way, she observed the author's question–answer routine. Sanda altered the author's words, however, by negating the adult's response, especially when it did not jibe with the original words, and instead contributed her own interpretation.

This reenactment involved Sandra's construction of the story guided by the illustrator's visual cues and an internalization of some of the adult's patterns for reading aloud. She assumed the role of the narrator as well as the person who delivers the story to a listener. Thus, the reenactment illustrates how she processed the words and pictures of the author's text as well as the performance cues of the adult reader's text.

### Written Sequels

Unlike retellings and reenactments, in which readers reproduce an author's information in some manner, writing sequels place different demands on the reader. In writing the continuing story of Pecos Bill, for example, students in Annyce's second-grade class demonstrated an awareness of basic genre conventions, text structure, character–event relationships, tone, and style, among other features.

In one lesson, Annyce explicitly emphasized the genre characteristic of tall tales as "stretching the truth." Although not explicit in the lesson, she included this activity in a unit on folktales featuring characters with a dominant but limited range of traits. In this event, Annyce read a storybook entitled *Pecos Bill Finds a Horse* to her second-grade class in a folktale unit (Golden & Gerber, 1990). Before reading, she discussed the concept of "stretching the truth," in which you tell a tall tale about a character's adventures. During the reading of the tale, Annyce periodically paused to invite the children's comments on the adventures, especially in relation to whether the truth was being stretched, as in the following exchange:

| | |
|---|---|
| Teacher: | *Do you think that that would be possible for a cowboy to be on a mountain lion?* |
| Students: | *No.* |
| Student: | *It's make-believe.* |
| Student: | *No. They stretched it out.* |

After the reading of the text, Annyce announced: "What we're going to do is make a big chapter [book] out of all the different episodes of Pecos Bill … kinds of other adventures Pecos Bill could have … write words to describe stretching the truth." After a brainstorming session about possibilities, the children chose to work individually, in pairs, or in groups to write their chapters.

*Marie's Text.*    Marie wrote the following narrative:

*Pecos Bill found a cat. He said, "Do you want some meat?" The little cat ran away. Pecos Bill started walking. In a few minutes he saw the eagle flying in the air. Pecos Bill jumped the eagle. They were flying in the air. Pecos Bill called him "Flying Cowboy." He went to this ranch and saw a bull. He ran to his eagle and flied west. He saw the bull and eagle flew on the bull. The bull started running away. By the time he got home, the bull was chasing him. He tied his eagle and went inside to sleep.*

*In the morning his eagle was gone. Half of the rope was laying on the ground. He went to go look for another animal to ride. He made a trap of buffalo meat and the bull came and Pecos Bill jumped on the bull and asked him if he could be his partner. The bull said "yes." Then he went to his house. They went to sleep.*

*The next morning they went riding. While they were riding, they saw the cat and the eagle. They said, "Do you want to be Pecos Bill's pets?" They said "yes."*

*The next month the cat had babies. They all went riding on the eagle. And the eagle made a nest for seven cats. They were in Pecos Bill's house. The seven cats went to sleep.*

*Next month, the eagle had babies. So the eagle had to make more nests. The bull went to sleep, even the eagle and the cat, even Pecos Bill. They lived happily ever after.*

Writing a sequel, as Marie did in the preceding example, required her to illustrate the exaggerated abilities of the character and to distort believability. Marie did not replicate the events as relayed in the author's text, but generated different events while maintaining the generic conventions of tall tales. Her new tale paralleled the original in that the basic topic focused on how Pecos Bill acquired new pets. Instead of a horse and a mountain lion, she selected an eagle, a bull, and cats. The abilities of the animals and Bill were similar to those in the original in that Bill could ride on an unusual animal (i.e., an eagle) and the animals worked together to create a family because he had lost his own. Yet, the new characters are consistent with their own traits, such as the eagle, which flies and builds nests. The dominant spirit is cooperative rather than antagonistic. Marie's tale works as a sequel, then, by maintaining the exaggerated abilities of the characters, thereby stretching the truth.

### Storytelling

When we examine the nature of the relationship between the author's text and the storyteller's rendition, aspects of performance can provide some clues to how the student interprets the story. The audience can discern the teller's stance toward the narrative, interpretation of characters, perceptions of what is suspenseful and climactic, views of moral actions, and so forth. As tales are passed along, each telling creates a new text, illustrating the living, growing nature of narrative. The function of the text also changes, depending on the context in which the tale is told.

Tales can function to perpetuate an oral history or a cultural tradition, to instruct youth, or to entertain, among other functions. Storytelling is essentially a communication event in which the performer conveys a story to an audience. It is communication, not in the sense of transmitting a message with a meaning, but rather in terms of presenting a verbal display to the listener that guides him or her in constructing a story world. Bauman (1986) described the performance as the "enactment of the poetic function, the essence of spoken artistry" (p. 3).

The storytelling events discussed in this section were part of a 6-week program in which preservice teachers worked with intermediate grade students from an urban school to transform folktales and myths from written to oral forms (Green & Golden, 1983). After discussing, selecting, and, in some cases, rewriting versions of folktales, pairs or groups of students worked on presenting their tale in an oral mode to their peers. Performances were videotaped for the students' review. Excerpts from the performances of three students are used to illustrate what storytelling can show about students' interpretation of narrative. In the left column, the students' words are noted and in the right column, his or her nonverbal behaviors are described.

*James.* James, a fifth-grader, illustrated overgeneralization of nonverbal cues, relying heavily on kinesics to tell *Odyssey* (his version of *Persephone*), as is evident in the following segment:

| Words | Nonverbal |
|---|---|
| *Odyssey was very beautiful. She was the pride and joy of her mother Colus. Her hair was as long as a comet's tail and as bright as the heavens. Her eyes were like stars on a moonlit night, and her cheeks were red and rosy like fiery gems.* | Raised hands, emphasized *very*, looked up clasped hands to chest, touched *hair* and leaned back, looked up extended hands out to signal heavens *bright* eyes like stars—hands framed facial expression—circled hands show brightness, cheeks red and rosy turns hand and facial expressions bright, open. |

| | |
|---|---|
| *Meanwhile, Stom, the evil magician, sat thinking on his throne a plot to get Odyssey. He had flipped his comet. He was definitely head over heels in love. So he charted his course and sped off to the meteor, Cosmos, the Jartan's leader: As Stom neared the meteor the Jartan's leader stepped out from behind his throne. He was chewing Hubba Bubba bubble gum and juggling three hot dogs. He dropped one. He started juggling them again. He dropped another one. He held on to the last hot dog. Stom pleaded with the Jartan's leader for the hand in marriage of Odyssey. In the middle of his first and last hot dog, Cosmos looked down on the pleading magician and agreed, something he would later regret.* | Sat down quickly and firmly, looked down, changed voice to show dissonance of Stom thinking of a plot. |
| | When Stom pleaded, James looked up, clasped hands. Cosmos looked down—James looked down. |
| | Paused—set fingers apart and pointed. |

To emphasize how Odyssey was the pride and joy of her mother, James looked up and clasped his hands to his chest. He touched his hair, leaned back, and looked up to signal how Odyssey's hair was as long and bright as the heavens. When James talked about Odyssey's eyes like stars, he used an open facial expression and formed his hands into circles held near his eyes.

James shifted his body to convey a change in character and tone of the story when Stom the evil magician was introduced. He sat down abruptly and looked down at the floor, as Stom might look down disapprovingly from the planet above.

James also used paralanguage to interpret the story. He emphasized that Odyssey was *very* beautiful by stressing and elongating the word. He also stressed words such as *hair*, *bright*, and *cheeks* to illustrate the qualities of Odyssey. His intonation patterns and tone changed as he shifted to Stom's perspective. He lowered his voice to reflect the angry tone of the evil magician. The paralanguage and kinesics were readjusted when James focused on Cosmos, the Jartan leader, who was chewing bubble gum. James' face showed an open expression; his body movements grew more fluid; and he pretended to chew the bubble gum.

These interpretations convey a sense of humor in an otherwise serious tale. This humor is not characteristic of this myth, thus illustrating how the individual reader's interpretation of the text creates a new tale.

*Kathy.* James' rendition is in contrast to the style used by Kathy, a fourth-grader, in her telling of McGovern's *Too Much Noise* as seen in the following segment:

| Words | Nonverbal |
|---|---|
| *Then Peter went back to the wise man, and the wise man said, "Get a dog and a cat." Peter said, "What good is a dog and a cat anyhow." So all day the dog said "ruff ruff." All day the cat said "meow meow." All day the sheep said "baa." All day the hen said "cluck cluck." All day the donkey said "hee-haw." All day the cow said "moo." The bed creaks. The floor squeaks. The leaves fall on the roof.* | Stressed get a dog and cat. Inflected voice for question; shrugged shoulders, raised arms to show resignation. "Ruff ruff" emphasized "meow" softened to sound like cat. "Cluck cluck" sound for hen. "Baa" sound for sheep. "Hee-haw"—pitch raised. "Moo" elongated. "Creak" sounds like creak. Squeaks—high pitch—jumps from floor. Shhhh sand waves arms back and forth. Blow Whistle/sways. |
| *The wind flows. The leaves blow on the roof. Ah, then Peter was angry. He went back to the wise man and said, "My house is too noisy. You told me to get a dog. All the dog does is 'ruff ruff.' You told me to get a cat.* | Stressed then Peter was angry, stomps feet, purses lips. Intonation patterns reflected anger of character—tone mentioned throughout, reflecting exasperation of character. |
| *All day the cat says 'meow meow.' You told me to get a hen. All day the hen says 'cluck cluck.' You told me to get a sheep. All day the sheep says 'baa.' You told me to get a donkey. All day the donkey says 'hee-haw.' You told me to get a cow. All day the cow goes 'moo.'"* | |

| | |
|---|---|
| *Peter was so angry that he said—he was so angry at the wise man he said, "What can I do?" The wise man says, "I can help you. Let the dog go, the cat go, the hen go, the donkey go, the sheep go, the cow go." So Peter let the hen go, the dog go, the cat go, the sheep go, the donkey go, and the cow go. Ah, what a quiet—the bed—no more dog saying "ruff ruff." No more cat saying "meow meow." No more hen saying "cluck cluck." No more sheep saying "baa." No more donkey saying "hee-haw." No more cow saying "moo." Ah, the bed creaked. Ah what a quiet noise. The floor squeaked. Ah, what a quiet noise. The leaves fell on the roof, the wind blew. The tea kettle whistled. Ah, oh what a quiet noise. And Peter went to bed and dreamed a very, very quiet dream.* | Angry tone disappears when wise man speaks. Angry tone is emphasized again when Peter speaks. Slowed down, softened tone, elongated advice.

Peter's tone has lost its anger.

Softened voice when saying "quiet noise." Speech slowed—reflects tone of relief, and *very, very quiet* is stressed—ends saying *quiet dream* softly and drops to the floor. |

Kathy, like James, relied on the use of kinesics as a way of interpreting the story. Kathy, however, memorized the author's words rather than construcing a version. In this case, movements were planned with her partner Amy to execute a certain pattern that illustrated the sound elements conveyed in the text. For example, when the text indicated that the wind blew and leaves fell on the roof, she swayed her body back and forth and moved her arms. She jumped in the air to emphasize how the floor squeaked. In addition, when the character went to the wise man and heard his suggestions, Kathy shrugged her shoulders to indicate the character's surprise at the advice.

Paralanguage is also evident in the performance. To convey the sounds of the animals, Kathy mimicked the sounds of the animals by elongating the sound. The cow's "moo" was low and drawn out. The donkey's "hee-haw" was high-pitched and clipped. She also differentiated between the narrative of the story and the dialogue between the characters. She reflected Peter's angry tone when he addressed the wise man and his tone of resignation when he decided to do what he was told. Intonation patterns in the dialogue segments thus were more varied to reflect the characters' reactions.

As the telling wound to a close and the house became quieter, Kathy's voice grew softer, the tempo slowed, and the relief of the character was reflected in her voice. As the character fell asleep, she lowered herself to the floor, and curled up just as the character might have done.

*Sally.*   In the final example, Sally, a fourth-grader, displayed less nonverbal behavior, partly because of her reliance on the author's text:

| Words | Nonverbal |
|---|---|
| *Atlanta, a swift huntress, was famous for her beauty and courage. Many young men came to woo her. She steadfastly refused to marry. Her father was not of the same mind, however. For a long time, he urged his daughter to marry.* | She looked down at note cards. She did not display eye contact. Her intonation pattern did not vary noticeably. The rate of delivery was fairly fast as if trying to report from memory. |
| *Finally, losing all of his patience, he insisted she pick one of her suitors. Atlanta did not want to get married but she decided that she would challenge her father. But this means she would try to avoid marriage but if it did persist, she would rely on her speed to help her.* | The student sat in a chair and had limited body movement. |

Sally read from note cards occasionally, and when she looked up, her body was set in one position, her eyes focused directly on the camera. Her intonation patterns were not varied. They suggested the tone that often accompanies the reading aloud of a story without verbal expression. As stated earlier, this behavior relates to the dependency on the author's text, but with more experience and perhaps a simpler tale, the child could free herself up to interpret the text nonverbally.

## Journals

Journal responses to books reveal the texts that students read and how they respond to them. Journal responses show students' preferred types of responses, such as relating incidents in the story or judging the quality of the story, and how responses vary across different texts as well as within texts. It is possible to gain insights into how students construct, interpret, and find significance in narratives by looking at their journal responses.

Examples from Diane's journal are used to illustrate how she responded to different narratives. Students in Elaine's fifth-grade class wrote journal responses to books they selected for independent reading. Elaine responded to students' entries through dialogic comments and questions (Golden & Handloff, 1993).

*Diane.*   Over a 3-month period, Diane responded to seven novels representing a range of genres such as modern fantasy, contemporary realism, biography, and historical fiction. She often wrote several entries on one book, thereby responding as the narrative unfolded. Her responses reflected the narrative at a particular point rather than as a reaction to a completed narrative. In her response to Burnett's *Little Princess*, Diane revealed several ways that she linked into the text. In the first part of one entry, Diane translated information from the author's text:

> *Sara was dressed in her very pretty furs when she saw a girl about her age, only she was in rags peering through the railing.*

In the next section, Diane offered a personal observation on the situation of the character as well as an interpretation of how the character is treated:

> *I think it isn't fair if a girl has to work very hard, gets scarcely any food, and is treated like scum!*

Her interpretation of a second character's trait of snobbery is illustrated by an example of the character's action. This response shows how Diane is formulating a conception of a character based on her interpretation of events:

> *I really think Lavina, the eldest of the girls, is a snob. Lavina doesn't let less fortunate children share her wealth. Becky is the servant girl that Sarah saw speaking through the railing.*

In one comment, Diane revealed her interpretation of a trait of Sarah's and a personal reaction to the event in which Becky cannot hear the story:

*Sarah tells the most breathtaking stories, so I think Becky should have been able to hear the story too.*

In the final part of the entry, Diane assessed the literary quality of the narrative in her comments on the author's style of writing:

*I do admire Burnett's work; it is very flowing, exciting, and loving.*

In one of several journal entries on Bulla's *Pocahontas and the Strangers*, Diane also revealed how she was constructing the narrative. In the first part of the entry, she discussed a particular event involving John Smith and Pocahontas and her reactions to the event. The comments indicate how she is both translating and responding to textual information:

*I have been surprised the Indians wanted to kill Captain John Smith but Pochohontas didn't want him to die. I think she did the right thing, when he was near death she said "do not hurt him, for he is mine." Now she has John Smith.*

In the next part of the entry, Diane interpreted a character's feelings and provided observations regarding what happened in the story to support her interpretation. In her final statement, she analyzed the character's actions in relation to the aforementioned event involving John Smith:

*I think Pochohontas felt sorry for the Englishmen, they didn't know how to hunt, or grow wheat and corn, so Pochohontas gathered all of the children and went to the storehouse to get lots of food for the English-men. I really do think Pochohantas's good thinking saved the Englishman's life.*

In her entry on Clark's *Freedom Crossing*, Diane also engaged in translating and interpreting information. In the first portion of her entry, she focused on how a character is escaping from slavery and predicted whether he would make it to safety:

*I now am reading the part were Martin (a young slave in hiding) is going to cross the border to Canada where slaves are free. It's very dangerous, many slave-catchers hide right near the border, they will probably catch the slave, beat him or even kill him and arrest the white people who helped to try and get the slave to safety across the border.*

In the second portion of the entry, Diane shifted from predicting what would occur based on information she has previously read to projecting herself into the situation of the character. This identification also is based on textual information regarding the treatment of slaves:

> If I were a slave I'd feel as if someone caught me and made me work all day, give me hardly enough food to live on, and if you tried to runaway you'd be shot! I hope Martin will be free in Canada and many more slaves too.

Diane's journal responses indicated a range of links with authors' texts. She translated characters and events with reference to the authors' messages, and she integrated information and made inferences about narrative elements. Her "texts" reflected personal reactions to the narratives and the way authors revealed these worlds. Furthermore, she related personally to some characters, noting what their experiences signified for her.

## BRIDGING THEORY INTO PRACTICE

In the preceding discussion, the reader's reactive text is a focal point for exploring the role of the reader in constructing, interpreting, and signifying narrative texts. Distinctions are made between the author's text and the reader's text, with the observation that no one reader's construction stands as the correct parallel to an author's text. An author's text is always transformed into a story by a reader so that the reader's view of the world influences the nature of the story world.

A distinction also is made between the reader's tacit and articulated text. It is shown that the latter text represents a partial text, a glimpse into the story world the reader created. The analyses show that readers' texts can provide valuable insights into their storymaking abilities and processes.

In examining how participants engage in textual processes, analyze students' reactive texts in a particular classroom for indications of their storymaking abilities.

- Consider the types of reactive texts.

  What reactive texts are used in the classroom?
  Are certain reactive texts valued over others?

- Consider the students' production of reactive texts.

  Are some reactive texts easier for students to produce than others?
  Do particular students favor some reactive texts over others?

- Consider how reactive texts are evaluated.

  How is a student's reactive text compared with the author's text?
  How is one student's reactive text compared with another's?
  What does a reactive text suggest about the student's storymaking abilities?
  How is growth in storymaking ability measured?

# 6

# Intertextuality in Text and Discourse

> In this chapter, the interest is in exploring multiple narrative events in the same classroom for the purpose of understanding the nature of intertextuality. Analyses focus on intertextual links between narrative texts and storymaking events in a first-grade classroom. The emphasis is on some of the properties in texts that connect them to other texts, and on some of the properties in the discourse of events that connect them to other events.

From a social semiotic perspective, intertextuality entails the connections between narratives constructed during the event and previous (historical) texts, between reactive texts, and between the discourse events in which the texts are embedded. The property of intertextuality suggests that there is an aspect of one text and/or event that carries over to another text and/or event.

Intertextuality is defined by Fairclough (1992) as "the property texts have of being full snatches of other texts which may be explicitly demarcated or merged and which the text may assimilate, contradict, ironically echo, and so forth" (p. 84).

All meaning is intertextual because all texts are read against the background of other texts (Lemke, 1995). The background of texts comprises, in part, contradictory opinions, points of view, and value judgments (Bakhtin, 1986). Texts are read against the background of other texts, readers' reactive texts against other reactive texts, and discourse events against other events. Each community determines which texts are valued, which texts will serve as the backdrop for others, and how interpretive conventions will occur during discourse processes (Lemke, 1995).

## FROM TEXT TO TEXT

Intertextuality between narratives can be seen on a very general level against the backdrop of other narratives. That is, texts calling forth the process of narrativity are linked. Texts also can connect on the basis of shared genre characteristics and the specific demands of narrativity placed on the reader. For example, we read certain genres, such as fairy tales (depending on our interpretive community), in similar ways with similar expectations. We anticipate flat, static characters representing types (e.g., hero), distant times, progressive plots, motifs related to magic, and so forth. In addition, we read works by particular authors similarly. For instance, C. S. Lewis, Robin McKinley, and J. R. R. Tolkein, lead us to expect the classic hero pattern when reading their novels (Campbell, 1949).

Intertextuality involves not only how prior texts contribute to an existing chain of texts, but also the texts that interpreters bring to meaning-making processes (Fairclough, 1992). Consonant with this view, is the notion that each textual (re)production is "a new, unrepeatable event in the life of the text, a new link in the historical chain of speech communication" (1935, p. 106).

## FROM EVENT TO EVENT

Intertextuality also entails the properties that link one discourse event to another. When we participate in an activity, such as reading a text, we connect it to other reading events that have preceded it so that one event makes sense against the background of other events. Therefore, as the school year progresses, a historical chain of reading events evolves. Links between events can be viewed in terms of social and academic rules and expectations.

Intertextuality related to social expectations concerns how to do story in particular contexts, that is, observing rules for participation and turn-taking, understanding how to sit appropriately, knowing how to listen, and so on. Denise's admonition to students to "show me your best listening" implies that this "best listening" was defined in an earlier event (see chap. 3). Thus, one story event may invoke a previously established set of rules. A teacher's academic expectations governing textual events also can carry over from one event to another. Furthermore, expectations for students to engage in textual processes such as constructing, interpreting, and signifying texts also are evident across reading events. Links also can appear across events involving rejoinder texts, that is, procedures for conducting small group interpretations of stories (see chaps. 4 and 5). Text production and interpretation, then, are processes embedded in sociocultural discourse practices (Fairclough, 1995), and these practices reflect intertextual links within classroom contexts.

Consistent with the perspective presented here, intertextuality is a "multitiered" phenomenon in which text, event, and language link into each other during an interaction that is dialogic in nature (Bloome & Egan-Robertson, 1983).

## INTERTEXTUALITY BETWEEN TEXTS
## AND EVENTS IN VIVIAN'S CLASSROOM

Illustrative events providing the focus for analysis are selected from Vivian's first-grade classroom. Vivian, an African American, taught students who were primarily from White working class and aid-dependent families. In addition, there were three students from India whose second language was English, two African Americans, and one Chinese American (Davis & Golden, 1994).

A central focus in Vivian's class was to develop students' literacy by engaging them in a range of discourse processes for different purposes. Vivian incorporated into her curriculum a variety of genres including folktales, modern fairy tales, contemporary realism, and science fiction as well as scientific and historical information books, biographies, and poetry. Texts were presented through oral, written, and visual channels. Students participated in storymaking processes in a variety of ways that centered on producing, constructing, (re)constructing, interpreting, and signifying narratives.

Producing stories occurred during the spontaneous sharing of personal narratives and in the writing of topic-based and topic-open stories. The process of constructing narratives was visible mostly during group rug time when Vivian read aloud a text and engaged the children in discussing various aspects of the story including character, events, and narrator. In constructing stories, students were engaged in such activities as writing biographies, rewriting fairy tales with different endings, interpreting narrative through drama, performing legend dances, and reciting poetry.

To examine intertextual links in Vivian's classroom, relationships between several storybook events are examined. In terms of participants' interactions, the basic relationships were similar across events. Vivian structured the event assuming the roles of orchestrator, mediator, and validator of student and author participants in accordance with the social and academic expectations she established for the lesson. Her students assumed the primary role of responding to the teacher's queries or, at times, generating their own. The author's texts provided cues that guided narrative construction. *Participant roles* were either explicit as stated in the lesson or implicit, suggesting the students' prior knowledge of their roles.

Vivian basically structured the *teacher–student–author interactions* to occur before, during, and after the storymaking process. From observations of these interactions, it is possible to see the social and academic aspects that were highlighted during the events and to observe how these aspects connected to those in other events.

Vivian's social expectations for events were that students would observe the rules for participating in group (e.g., turn-taking, attentiveness). Her *academic expectations for the students* were that they would construct narrative elements and make personal connections with the story. Vivian's goals, in part, were to orient the students into mainstream literacy via the storybook reading discussion and to accept their "ways with words" in this process. The channels for the events were oral (teacher's performance of the author's text and participants' discussion of text), written (author's words) and visual (illustrator's images).

Although teacher–student–author interactions focused on the construction of meaning, different emphases were evident across some events (e.g., constructing, interpreting, signifying). In addition to intertextual links between channels, functions, and social and academic expectations, intertextual links were evident in terms of text level features including author-illustrator (e.g., Keats' stories illustrated in colláge and oil), literary elements of character (e.g., Keats' Peter stories), genres such as fantasy (e.g., *The Pied Piper of Hamlin* and *The Ugly Duckling*), topics such as dinosaurs (e.g., *Patrick's Dinosaurs* and *The Amazing Dinosaurs*), structure such as cumulative tales (e.g., versions of *The Little Red Hen*), and themes such as the individual's role of responsibility in ecology (e.g., class lesson on ecology and *Just a Dream*). A key point is that intertextuality is an outgrowth of the interaction among participants rather than a preestablished quality within the author's text.

## INTERTEXTUALITY BETWEEN EVENTS

Consistent with a social semiotic perspective, intertextuality in Vivian's classroom is viewed in terms of connections between textual features and between social discourse features. Each type of event was linked according to the structure of the event. That is, an author's work was presented orally by the teacher and participants engaged in the processes of constructing, interpreting and signifying texts. Vivian initiated the event and scaffolded the discussion. Students assumed the roles of respondents to Vivian's queries or offered spontaneous responses to the author's words and the illustrators' pictures.

Another type of link was that of the text embedded in the discourse (e.g., works by Ezra Jack Keats). One prominent way that Vivian established connections was to review a previously constructed text and event and use these to frame current ones (e.g., "Yesterday, we read one version of *The Ugly Duckling*; today we will compare it to another version").

The next section focuses on analyses of several picture storybook reading events, with particular emphasis on social expectations for participation and academic expectations for narrative construction. First, segments of three events are analyzed according to these expectations and the intertextual references to preceding and subsequent events. Thereafter, intertextual links across several events are examined in light of these same expectations.

## STORY EVENT 1: *THE SNOWY DAY*

Several narrative events in Vivian's classroom pertained to three picture storybooks written and illustrated by Ezra Jack Keats. In the first event involving one of his works, Vivian gathered the students for rug time, held up *The Snowy Day* (1962) and prefaced the story reading event in the following way:

> *Remember, I told you we were going to start a series of books by Ezra Jack Keats and that, not to persuade you or influence you in any way, E, but he is one of my favorite authors, and I will reading a series of his books and you're going to be noticing some distinct things about his books. The first book that we're going to read by Ezra Jack Keats is entitled what?*

This opening indicated forthcoming intertextual links reflecting the texts of one author and "distinct things" about his books. That is, it prepared the students to expect that connections among his texts would be recognized.

Before reading the text, Vivian stated: "Show me that you're ready to listen ... I'm ready to listen." She announced that she would read the book first and the discussion would follow. In reading the book, Vivian read the words first, then held up the pictures.

The discussion at the end focused on inferring information not explicitly stated by the words. Questions were asked that engaged the students in critical thinking, such as "Why didn't Peter know during the night that it was snowing?" A discussion ensued on whether snow makes noise when it falls.

In addition, students studied picture clues to interpret whether the snow seemed shallow or deep. Vivian also asked them to contribute words other than the author's "crunch, crunch, crunch" to convey the sound of walking in the snow. One student asked why the author wrote the word "s-l-o-w-l-y" in this way, prompting an activity that involved students in writing different words to represent their meaning graphically. Vivian introduced the final phase of the discussion in the following way:

> *Look at this picture. What does this picture make you think of? When I get this picture, I have a certain feeling. How do you feel? (she motioned for a child to be quiet). S?*

Students offered various responses including sad, happy, and mad. At the end of the discussion, the following exchange occurred:

| | |
|---|---|
| Teacher: | *How do you feel?* |
| Abby: | *Small.* |
| Teacher: | *Small? Is that what you're saying? That's so interesting. Why do you feel small? Shh, listen, I'm interested in Abby, listen.* |
| Abby: | (inaudible) |
| Teacher: | *Oh, because he looks so small in this big background of snow. Look at that—that's a very interesting comment. She feels small when she sees it. You can tell that here's a wide open area of snow and just this one little boy playing. I felt kind of lonely when I saw it. When I saw this picture I said, "Oh, it makes me feel kind of lonely. He's all by himself.* |
| Teacher: | *Do you think he might have felt lonely or small or sad? Could have been a lot of feelings we don't know any—there are no right or wrong answers. . . .* |

The preceding dialogue suggests that one of Vivian's interests was in eliciting students' personal responses to literature by encouraging them to relate their feelings to the work. She also contributed her own responses to the work.

## STORY EVENT 2: *THE SNOWY DAY AND HI, CAT!*

### Segment 1

A second event on the day after the reading and discussion of Keats' *The Snowy Day* showed Vivian engaging the students in exploring similarities and differences between the Ezra Jack Keats' texts, and in observing a rule for turn-taking:

| | |
|---|---|
| Teacher: | *Boys and girls, it's very, very important—we've talked about listening for certain kinds of things when we're reading stories. I want you to listen to these stories and keep in mind—keep in mind that there will be—there will be—there will be ideas brought out in the story that are similar to the—un—the—another story you've heard by Ezra Jack Keats (i.e., **The Snowy Day**), and they'll be ideas brought out in the story that are quite different from a—a previous story that we've read by Ezra Jack Keats, so keep those things in mind as we are listening to the two stories. Now remember, we read **The Snowy Day** and who was the main character? Raise your hand; do not call out. That's the one thing I'm trying to get you to do (she turns and shakes her finger at one child) to always raise your hands and not call out. You always have super answers, but you can't them—call out, and it's not our rule—remember our rule (she sits down). All right, who's the main character in **A Snowy Day**? Ty, who's the main character?* |
| Ty: | *Peter.* |
| Teacher: | *I can't hear you babe.* |
| Ty: | *Peter.* |
| Teacher: | *Peter, yes. The main character in the story, **A Snowy Day**, is Peter (she writes Peter on the board). And what did we decide—did we decide about the story **A Snowy Day**? About the character in the story? Do you remember?* |
| Katy: | *Um ... the ... um ... boys were playing ... um ... a snowfight.* |
| Teacher: | *Okay, but no, what did we decide about the number of characters in the story **The Snowy Day**?* |
| Carol: | *There weren't that many.* |
| Teacher: | *We realized that there weren't that many characters in that particular story, and what else did we did we decide? Do you remember?* |
| Nat: | (inaudible.) |
| Teacher: | *Yes, what about that character Peter? What about Peter?* |
| Randy: | *He was—he was—he went outside. And these two boys were ... uh ... doing the snowfight but he (decided) not to do it.* |
| Teacher: | *Okay, well we decided he was obedient, didn't we? He had been told not to play with the bigger ...* |
| Students: | *... boys.* |
| Teacher: | *... boys. So we decided he was obedient.* |

| | |
|---|---|
| Bart: | *Um ... um ... Peter couldn't play with the boys because he was—he—he ... um ... said to hisself—'cause he's too little.* |
| Teacher: | *Okay, and he had been. Who do you think told him not to play with the big boys?* |
| Gary: | *His mom.* |
| Teacher: | *His mom, and that's why we decided Peter was obedient, okay?* (writes "was obedient" on the board) *What else? Do you remember? Um ... I just see the two hands. A?* |
| Abby: | *Because—because his mom told him he was too young.* |
| Teacher: | *Alright. That goes with the fact that he's obedient.* |

In the first part of the segment, Vivian explicitly stated that the purpose of the event was to listen for similarities and differences in stories written by Ezra Jack Keats. She made an implicit intertextual link to other events (apart from Keats' works) by stating that "we've talked about listening for certain kinds of things when we're reading stories."

As Vivian began to review characters in *The Snowy Day*, she articulated the rule for turn-taking, that is, raising your hand and not calling out. Her admonition to "remember our rule" implies a link to expectations for turn-taking established in previous events.

In the remaining part of the segment, Vivian guided the students in constructing a trait of the character (i.e., he was obedient). Ostensibly, then, Vivian steered the discussion toward a group consensus regarding Peter's character. At the end of the segment, Vivian referred to this trait as a "fact" about Peter, a fact established by the readers rather than explicitly stated in the text. In other words, participants "decided" that Peter was obedient instead of identifying a "correct" meaning from the text. This trait was not explicitly stated in the text and therefore was inferred by the participants. This segment suggests that Vivian perceived interpretation as shared meaning.

Similarly, in the following exchange, Vivian reminded the students about their decision regarding how characters were feeling:

| | |
|---|---|
| Teacher: | *Alright, we decided that he didn't always like to be ...* |
| Students: | *... alone.* |
| Teacher: | *Alone, he liked playing more with a* |
| Students: | *Friend.* |
| Teacher: | *Friend. He liked playing with a friend* (writes on board) *instead of what?* |
| Students: | *Being alone.* |
| Teacher: | *Instead of being alone. And you know what, there are times when it's good to be alone, and Peter did do that. He played alone, but he* |

> *decided that the next time I play out in the snow I'd rather be with a ...*
>
> Students: *Friend.*
> Teacher: *Friend. He liked playing with a friend.*

Two new patterns are evident in the preceding segment. Vivian paused at the end of a sentence, and the students completed the answer in unison. Vivian confirmed their answers orally and by writing them on the board. In addition, Vivian provided her own interpretation of good behavior when she commented that "sometimes it's good to be alone."

In another line of questioning, Vivian distinguished between the two kinds of answers she wanted: "Okay, what—a—I mean—we can imagine that he doesn't like being alone, but what do we actually know about him?" In response to this, students generated answers, which Vivian confirmed: "Alright, he has a name of a boy. We've seen a picture of him in the story—this shows that he is a boy. That's something we know, the information is right there. We know that he's a boy; we know that he is little.

In a final line of questioning, Vivian asked the students: "But what was something that we really, really noticed about Peter because of something he did? We decided something very important about him because of something he did in the story. Do you remember?" The students discussed how he put the snowball in his pocket. Vivian responded: "So we decided that he didn't know too much about snowballs?" Students speculated that he might not have known about this because he did not know about snow or because he was very young. Vivian confirmed these responses, adding that there could have been a lot of responses.

There are intertextual links between events 1 and 2 illustrated in the preceding dialogue. As in the case of deciding on the trait "obedient," Peter was depicted as liking to play with a friend. In the latter section, Vivian offered a judgment that "there are times when it's good to be alone, and Peter did do that." This suggests not only a link to the previously read text, but also to a feature of discourse that Vivian pursued in subsequent events, that is, a judgment of appropriate behavior: "there are times when it's good to be alone."

## Segment 2

After the review of *The Snowy Day*, Vivian held up *Keats' Goggles* (1969) and *Hi Cat!* (1970), stating: "Now, look at these two books. Alright, what can you tell me about these two books just by looking at the covers?"

After a brief discussion, students directed by Vivian observed that the books were by the same author and featured the same characters, including Peter. As in the previous event, Vivian announced how she would structure the event:

| | |
|---|---|
| Teacher: | *I want to read to you first. This—**Hi Cat!** I'm going to read it through without discussing it. And very very quickly because the dis—the story itself is very very easy to read. Both of the stories are easy to read. But I want to go over some similarities of the books and then see if they're similar to **The Snowy Day**. Remember, we said **The Snowy Day** seemed like a very lonely story with very few characters?* |

Vivian structured this event similarly to event 1, by reading the text and eliciting discussion afterward. In the first instance, topics of discussion initially began with inferring questions and a brief focus on vocabulary, then moved to graphic representation of words and finally to a discussion on emotional identification with the character. After this discussion, however, Vivian addressed issues related to the students' confusion about the characters that she noticed during the reading of the story:

| | |
|---|---|
| Teacher: | *You are rather confused about who these characters are. Now—shhh—listen to me very—if you're—you see you must be good listeners. First of all, you can't play* (she shakes her finger at them) *and be good listeners. You really have to listen. I'm going to read that very first page again, and you really need to listen.* |
| Student: | *Stop it.* (student is bothered by another child.) |
| Teacher: | *On his way, okay? Sit right, then you won't be kicking him in the back with your knees. Move back some more, 'cause you're deliberately doing that. On his way to meet Peter, Archie saw someone new on the block. Now, just by that sentence, on his way to meet Peter, Doug, Archie saw someone new on the block. Doug, who is this?* (she walks over and takes something from a child, and shows Doug the cover of the book.) |
| Doug: | *Peter.* |
| Teacher: | *Alright. You still think it's Peter. Who is this?* (she shows him the picture inside the book.) |
| Student: | *I don't know.* (whispered) |
| Student: | *I know, I know.* |
| Doug: | *Archie.* |

| | |
|---|---|
| Teacher: | *Archie. Can this be Peter and this be Archie?* (she shows him the two pictures of the same boy.) |
| Doug: | *Uh uh.* |
| Teacher: | *Well, who's what? What's—what's going on here? Who is this?* (refers to picture). |
| Doug: | *Archie.* |
| Teacher: | *Who is that?* (refers to cover picture) |
| Doug: | *Archie.* |
| Teacher: | *Archie. This is Archie, boys and girls. But you think of him as Peter because you saw us—we read a story called The Snowy Day. You see a brown boy who's young and you're thinking that it looks like* (she opens The Snowy Day to show them a picture of Peter) *Archie. But does this look like Archie?* |
| Students: | *No.* |
| Teacher: | *No.* |
| Steve: | *It's Peter.* |
| Teacher: | *This is Peter.* |
| Student: | *I know that.* |

In the first part of this segment, Vivian stated her expectations for good listening. First, she said, "You can't play." Later in the lesson, she retrieved an object with which a child was playing. A second expectation, which was implied, was that the children must listen carefully to clear up confusion about who the characters are. In addition to "good listening," the rule for group participation was "to sit right," as stated in response to a student's complaint, that is, to stay in your space and not kick another student.

To assist students in sorting out their confusion, Vivian suggested not only listening carefully, but also looking at the illustrations to clarify who the characters are. Here we can see another intertextual link in terms of reading strategies. In both segments, Vivian referred students to pictures to identify or interpret characters.

### Segment 3

In the final phase of the event, Vivian drew a Venn diagram on the board and discussed with the students what the circles looked like and how to use them for comparisons of Keats' texts:

| | |
|---|---|
| Teacher: | *All right. That's the circle for **Hi Cat!**. When we read **Goggles** this afternoon, we're going to find out who the main characters are. Do we almost know who the main characters are?* |

Students:  *Yes.* (students clapped)

Teacher:  *Just by the picture? Who did we say we thought the main characters were?*

Students:  *Archie and Willie and Peter.*

Teacher:  (nods) *This is my circle for* **Goggles**. *I'm going to put it in—uh—let's say green—make it Christmassy.* (inaudible teacher–student exchange) *Now we're going to—to find out if the main characters in* **Goggles** *are the same as the main characters in* **Hi Cat!**. *If they are the same, where will I be putting them, S?*

Student:  *In the same (shape).*

Teacher:  *In the same—almost—in the same what?*

Student:  *Circle.*

Teacher:  *Circle. In the same circle. We'll see if that's what's going to happen—that would show that these people have something in ...*

Student:  *Common.*

Teacher/
Students:  *Common.*

Teacher:  *And I always say that to you, don't I? What do they have in common? What do they have that are just ...*

Students:  *Alike.*

Teacher:  *Alike. The same. We'll see. All right, we do have to stop.*

In the preceding interaction, Vivian signaled the activity she had planned for the afternoon, a comparison of a third Peter story by Keats, *Goggles*. She invited the students to predict the main characters, and ended by saying, "I always say that to you, don't I? What do they have in common?" In this way, Vivian made an instructional goal for constructing narrative explicit to the students. Moreover, by saying "I always say that to you," she suggested that this goal is an ongoing focus of discourse surrounding text. At the same time, she oriented them to the Venn diagram as a way of capturing similarities and differences between characters. Mention of the circle shape suggests that students may have previously studied the concept of shapes.

## STORY EVENT 3: *JUST A DREAM*

### Segment 1

Vivian and her students recapped information from a previous discussion about what each student could do to make the environment better (i.e., precycle, recycle, reuse, and reduce), thereby highlighting an intertextual link to theme while reestablishing social expectations for participation. After referring to the activity that would follow reading aloud the first part of *Just a Dream* (i.e., making earth buttons), Vivian began reading:

| | |
|---|---|
| Teacher: | *I don't want to hear anymore. I've already—I've already said—move over baby 'cause that's where you're supposed to be, okay? All right. Now. Hands down. No, Doug, I've called on you four times. I've given you your opportunity. Now. I'm going to read to you today, and we won't get finished, but I will read parts of it each—for the re—for the rest of this week. It's called* **Just a Dream**. (She shows them the cover.) *All right. Now. I will read part of it because then we have to make our what?* (She holds up the button papers.) |
| Students: | *Earth day buttons.* |
| Teacher: | *Our earth day buttons. Now. Shh. Are you ready? I'm ready. Shh. They aren't ready. You won't be making one if you aren't quiet. You won't make one at all. No. I don't want to hear you. If you make a comment, you're making just as much noise as the person I asked to be quiet.* **Just a Dream** *(1990) by Chris van Allsburg.* As usual, Walter stopped at the bakery on his way home from school. He bought one large jelly-filled doughnut. |
| Students: | *Mmmm.* |
| Teacher: | He took the pastry from its bag, eating quickly as he walked *(along)*. He licked the red jelly from his fingers. Then he crumpled up the empty bag and threw it by the fire hydrant. |
| Students: | *Oh oh!* |
| Teacher: | At home, Walter saw Rose, the little girl next door, watering a tree that had just been planted. *And what did I tell you about these trees?* |
| Student: | *We're going to make one.* |
| Teacher: | *We're going to plant one.* |
| Teacher/ Students: | *Plant one.* |
| Teacher: | *Plant a tree. And what else did I tell you about trees? Something that's real important. What should you do the next time you're going to be getting a gift?* |
| Students: | *Ooohhh.* |
| Teacher: | *Next time it's your birthday, or gifts. Yes, Doug?* |
| Doug: | *You could tell your mom or dad to get you a—a tree.* |

| | |
|---|---|
| Teacher: | *Don't you think that would be a nice birthday gift?* |
| Students: | *Yeah.* |
| Teacher: | *Or a nice gift for some other occasion. Instead of saying …* |
| Student: | *Or Christmas.* |
| Teacher: | *You could say, "Oh mom and dad, would you get me a tree that I could plant and I'll watch it grow?"* |
| Student: | *And that would be a—Mrs. xxx—also it would be a gift for the earth.* |
| Teacher: | *It would be a gift for the earth, and it would be a gift forever. Because you can outgrow the bikes, you can lose that bike; the bike can break up, some of them, in a couple of days.* |
| Student: | *Or they can—or they can get stolen.* |
| Teacher: | *As long as you take good …* |
| Teacher/ Students: | *Care of it …* |
| Teacher: | *It will be there for …* |
| Teacher/ Students: | *Ever.* |
| Teacher: | *As long as you want it to.* |
| Student: | *What if you cut it down?* |
| Teacher: | *As long—until you cut it down.* |
| Student: | *I have a … uh … apple tree.* |

In the first part of the exchange, Vivian focused on stating several expectations for social participation in the lesson: sitting where you're supposed to be, putting your hands down when the teacher is ready to read, and being quiet. In addition, Vivian commented to one student that he would not be called on because he had been called on several times before. Two of these examples pertaining to turn-taking suggest that raising one's hand does not always guarantee that you will be called on.

Academic expectations focused on a specific theme. The theme of contributing to the environment was reiterated from a previous lesson and the teacher asked, "What should you do the next time you're getting a gift?" This question, therefore, was prescriptive in nature, suggesting a specific, valued action that students should take.

### Segment 2

In this segment, Vivian returned to the story, framing it by inviting the students to learn whether the character acted according to her expectations for appropriate behavior:

| Teacher: | *Good. Alright, so listen. Let's see if Rose did as I suggested.* **Rose was watering her tree that had just been planted. Listen. "It's my birthday present," she said proudly.** *Rose and I think a—alike.* |
|---|---|
| Student: | *Same.* |
| Teacher: | **Walter couldn't understand why anyone would want a tree for a present.** *But Walter's not—he isn't thinking like us. Not yet. He isn't thinking like we do. Remember, he's the same guy who did what with the paper?* |
| Student: | *Threw it.* |
| Student: | *Threw it on the ground.* |
| Teacher: | *Threw it on the ground.* |
| Student: | *Near the hy—the fire hydrant.* |
| Teacher: | **His own birthday was just a few days away and he said, "huh, I'm not getting some dumb plant for a birthday." And he told that to Rose. She just shook her head** *(The teacher shows the picture.) Well, sometimes people aren't as aware of what the earth needs as we are. We're very much aware. But let's see if Walter …* |
| Students: | *Is aware.* |
| Teacher: | *Maybe he's going to …* |
| Student: | *Change to a nice boy.* |
| Teacher: | *Maybe he's going to change. If no one's ever talked to Walter about these things …* |
| Student: | *There a trash (can) near the fire hydrant.* |
| Student: | *He'll keep doing them.* |
| Teacher: | *He'll keep doing the same kinds of things.* |
| Student: | *There's a trash can by the fire hydrant.* |
| Teacher: | *But he—when someone talks to him about changing maybe he will, listen.* |

In the first part of the discussion, Vivian continued reading and sanctioned Rose's action by saying "we think alike." In this way, reader and character were personally linked. This strategy was similar to the discussion of *The Snowy Day* in terms of participants aligning themselves with the character. As the discussion progressed, Vivian continued to develop the theme by making the class participants superior to Walter because they know his actions are wrong.

In the middle of the segment, Vivian asked a recall question about Walter's action, and the students answered "threw it on the ground." Again,

Vivian positioned the character's action against their own, and participants speculated on whether Walter might change, agreeing that he might if he became aware. (An implicit goal of Vivian's was to make students conscious of their role in protecting the environment.) One student's response on the location of the trash can was not acknowledged.

## Segment 3

In the following segment, the participants discuss the results of people violating the recommendations for getting rid of trash by connecting the character's dream to the real world:

---

| | |
|---|---|
| Teacher: | *Even though it was a dream, who caused all that trash?* |
| Student: | *People* |
| Teacher: | *People. Thank you. People put that trash there. Animals didn't do it—like your dog or cat—they didn't put the trash there.* |
| Student: | *Or fish.* |
| Teacher: | *People like you or I. People like you and I, but they are people who are not thinking about our ...* |
| Teacher/ Students: | *Earth.* |
| Teacher: | *And how do we take care of it? But Walter was the main person who did not take care. He threw his trash everywhere. He didn't even sort the trash when he had the opportunity. So landfills, or for the trash they had to dig more landfills because one landfill was full—had to dig some place else—another landfill full—had to go someplace else, and people in the neighborhood were—started yelling, "I don't want a landfill in my neighborhood."* |
| Student: | *That's where Floral (neighborhood) is.* |
| Teacher: | *So here they are—where does the trash go?* |
| Students: | (inaudible) |
| Teacher: | *Now if people had been ...* (She points to the board.) |
| Teacher/ Students: | *Precycling, reusing, and recycling and reducing.* |
| Student: | *We wouldn't have all this mess.* |
| Teacher: | *Wouldn't have that mess. All right, we're going to stop and go with the rest of the story tomorrow.* |

---

Vivian framed the discussion by connecting Walter's dream of the future to a real-world problem of people creating the trash. Again, Vivian implied a difference between class participants who are aware and other people who are not. She summarized the problem to which Walter's actions led and directed the students to state the theme of the ecology lesson (written on the board), that is, precycling, reusing, recycling, and reducing. Intertextual links were established when the teacher indicated that they would continue with the story the next day. Vivian's discourse pattern of pausing so that students could fill in words (e.g., Teacher: … "not thinking about our …"; Students: "Earth") also is evident in the second event in which students completed Vivian's utterance (e.g., Teacher: "I'd rather be with a …"; Students: "Friend").

## STORY EVENT 4: *THE UGLY DUCKLING*

### Segment 1

In event 4, Vivian introduced a previously read version of *The Ugly Duckling* for the purpose of comparing it with another version, as in the focus of event 2 involving a comparison of works by Keats:

| | |
|---|---|
| Teacher: | *We were—we read this story of **The Ugly Duckling**, okay? In this story—this story is Hans Christian Andersen version—the original version of the story as it was written. Now remember, we said today we're going to hear another story of **The Ugly Duckling**, but this time we're going to listen to the story retold by another person, so we're going to see if this one is written just like …* |
| Student: | *Or different.* |
| Teacher: | *Or if it's different. Okay, … R's not ready. A isn't ready. Now she is. We're going to wait very quickly for J. Move faster, J, 'cause I want you over here when we start the story. While we're waiting, who can think of their favorite part of the story yesterday? Favorite, favorite part.* |

In this introduction, Vivian stated that the purpose of the event was to identify commonalities and differences between the two versions. A student added "or different," which Vivian confirmed. Thus, an intertextual link between events 2 and 4 in terms of academic expectations was made. Social expectations regarding the need to "sit right" are indicated in the second part when Vivian stated she should wait for J. Until the students were seated, Vivian engaged others in a filler discussion (i.e., divergent from the purpose of the event), focusing on their favorite part of the story.

## Segment 2

In this segment, Vivian centered the discussion on differences between how the two versions are told and illustrated, building on students' observations:

| | |
|---|---|
| Teacher: | *Now, I'm going to stop at this very, very early stage. Who remembers the beginning of this one* (displays Andersen version). *All right, Mindy?* |
| Mindy: | *Um—that um—the ... uh ... duck, the—it wasn't a big duck like that—it was a different color duck (sitting on her eggs), and they all hatched at one time.* |
| Teacher: | *All right, the illus ...* |
| Students: | *Noh—uh ...* |
| Teacher: | *Excuse me, shh, excuse me, the illustrations were different—let her—let her finish her thoughts. The illustrations were different, okay?* |
| Mindy: | *And ... um ... and only one didn't hatch and they—they—and ... em ... they had different colored beaks in that picture.* |
| Teacher: | *Okay. That's a difference, yes.* |
| Randy: | *Um, in the first part ... um ...* |
| Teacher: | *Da, shh* (whispered) |
| Randy: | *The duck doesn't say the same things in the other story.* |
| Teacher: | *Okay. The line—the—the conversation is different with the mother duck and the ducks, the ducklings. Okay.* |
| Student: | *The don't—they don't—in that story they don't talk about the, the, like—the castle.* |
| Teacher: | *Good for you.* |
| Doug: | *And that story—that story they—that story they talk about the castle and that story they don't.* |
| Teacher: | *Yes, that's what I noticed too, Doug. In this story, they described, in the very beginning the castle. It was so mu—the—the surroundings were so much in detail, they talked about the surroundings in this one. But in the beginning they get right to the heart of the story in this one, about the duckling. So this one seemed a bit more descriptive (a lot of descriptive language). You can make a decision, if you like one better than the other.* |

The social expectation for being quiet, especially when someone else is speaking was evident when Vivian said "Excuse me, shh," let her finish her thoughts. Later she whispered "shh" to a specific student. In terms of the academic expectations, Vivian asked a question about differences in the beginning of the story. Students responded in two ways: by noting differences in illustrations and in words. Vivian confirmed responses in the first instance and elaborated and named (descriptive) the differences noted in the second instance.

**Segment 3**

In the following exchange, the participants focused on experiences related to their and the character's actions of putting their heads under water:

---

Teacher:     Said the hen. "It's because you have nothing to do. Lay some eggs. Purr. Then you won't think about such silly things." "But it's so wonderful to swim," said the duckling. "But it's so wonderful to put your head underwater and dive down." *Right*?

Student:     *No.*

Student:     *That's fun down in the water.*

Teacher:     *(Just wondering if you were) paying attention.* "Wonderful?" cried the hen, "you must be crazy." (*Students laugh.*) "The cat is clever, ask him if he likes to swim. The old woman is wise, ask her if she likes to put her head underwater."

                  "You just don't understand," said the duckling. And they really didn't understand. The duckling was very correct on that point.

Student:     *I do put my head underwater sometimes.*

Student:     *I put my head underwater.*

Student:     *Everybody puts their—everybody puts their head underwater.*

Students:     (Talk at once.)

Teacher:     *But suppose—all right, shh, excuse me, freeze.*

Student:     *My sister don't.*

Teacher:     *Excuse me, freeze. Listen, okay? The argument is not whether or not you put your head underwater and your sister doesn't. Does that make your sister crazy because she doesn't?*

Student:     *No.*

Teacher:     *No it doesn't make her crazy. It just means she doesn't want to or she doesn't like to. It doesn't make her crazy. It's just—it just makes her different. Differences does not mean that the person is wrong, or*

> *crazy, or stupid* (students laugh). *I don't want to put my head un-*
> *derwater.*
> Student:    *Mrs. xxx.*
> Teacher:    *It's because I'm not a good swimmer.*
> Students:   (All talk at once.)
> Teacher:    *All right, freeze (please). One at a time. I need to hear you one at a*
> *time. Let's start with Abby.*

Students spontaneously offered their views and those of others about putting their heads under water and, at one point, they all talked at once. As in previous events, the students personally linked their experiences with those of the characters. In response, Vivian said, "Excuse me, freeze," not so much to get the students to speak one at a time, but rather to provide Vivian with the opportunity to get them on a different track. More specifically, she refocused them on how the characters scoffed at the duckling. This served as a basis for her to offer a value judgment about calling people crazy when they really are just different.

Values clarification also was apparent in events 2 and 3, which focused respectively, on being alone and taking responsibility for the environment. In the last utterance, Vivian used the same phrase, "all right, freeze." This enabled her to have the floor to talk—to invoke the rule of speaking one at a time.

## INTERTEXTUALITY BETWEEN EVENTS

### Social Expectations

Thus far, we have looked at intertextual links within and across three events in terms of social and academic expectations. In this section, the goal is to identify the principal intertextual links that illuminate these expectations in narrative events in Vivian's classroom.

In terms of social expectations, Vivian explicitly signaled the "rules" for participating in group storybook reading events on the rug. Three kinds of rules were evident:

1.    *Turn-taking.* Expectations for turn-taking focused primarily on students raising their hands to gain the floor and on ensuring that participants talked one at a time.

2.    *Attentiveness.* There were several ways that students were expected to display their attentiveness, each focusing on "showing you're ready." Stu-

dents were expected not to play with objects, not to talk to other classmates, and to listen politely while someone else was taking a turn. In addition to specifically stating the rules, Vivian also uttered "shh" and "excuse me" to maintain attention. In some cases, Vivian interrupted the flow of the event by naming a particular student or looking at an individual until he or she was attentive.

3.   *Sitting appropriately.* Several expectations regarding sitting were associated with demonstrating readiness for participation. Students had to be sitting in their particular space, sitting on their bottoms, sitting still and not touching other classmates. To express this rule, Vivian reminded the class on how to sit and addressed individual students who were not observing the accepted behavior. Sometimes she pointed to a student and motioned for him or her to sit down.

On occasion, Vivian reinforced the importance of listening to a particular student by drawing attention to the student and asking other participants to listen. This strategy served not only as a way to manage the discussion (e.g., "it is polite to listen when someone is speaking"), but also as a way of valuing of the student's viewpoint (e.g., "listen, J has an interesting point"; "You always have super answers but we can't hear them").

Raising one's hand, however, did not always guarantee a turn. Vivian was aware of distributing turn-taking so that one student did not have too many turns. This enabled all participants to have a voice. Hands were to go down when either a teacher or students had the floor. In addition, it was permissible for a student to offer a comment or question at times even if that student was not formally recognized. That is, a student could spontaneously respond to the story as it unfolded. Thus, the turn-taking rule generally was invoked when several participants talked at once and obscured individual responses. Thus, turn-taking rules essentially facilitated hearing an individual's voice.

## Academic Expectations

Academic expectations were evident in several ways across the three events: (a) referring to pictures for information, (b) constructing literary elements, (c) linking story with reader, and (d) using texts as a background for other texts.

1.   *Referring to pictures.* At several points, Vivian drew students' attention to pictures to highlight information relevant to constructing the narrative. Pictures were used to clarifying information (e.g., identify characters). Pictures also were used to specify information conveyed by the words (e.g.,

to show a particular aspect of a character's action). Pictures served to provide details for elaborating narrative elements (e.g., character traits, aspects of setting).

2. *Constructing literary elements.* Character construction was a major emphasis in the events. Vivian directed students in identifying character traits and considering whether characters changed these traits. Intertwined with the construction of character was the construction of theme. More specifically, characters' actions, particularly in the second and third events, were positively or negatively valued in explicit and implicit ways. These discussions seemed to work toward establishing a "group" consensus about the elements.

3. *Linking text with reader.* Vivian often focused the discussions at some point on connecting characters to readers. This is evident in several ways. Readers were encouraged to identify their own affective responses to events with those experienced by the character (e.g., "What emotions would you have felt?"). Readers were elevated to positions above the characters (e.g., "We are more aware of how to protect the environment than Walter"). Vivian led students in interpreting certain actions as more appropriate than others. In some instances, this indicated specific actions to follow (e.g., recycling) and, in others, specific ways of thinking about things (e.g., "people aren't crazy, just different"). With the exception of the first aforementioned instance above, Vivian established the connections between readers and text.

4. *Using text as a background for other texts.* A key pattern of intertextuality between events was evident when Vivian used texts and events to frame other texts and events. Framing included a variety of references to previous events, including textual strategies (i.e., comparing texts) and allusions to authors (i.e., Ezra Jack Keats) or narrative elements such as theme (i.e., taking responsibility for the environment).

## BRIDGING THEORY INTO PRACTICE

In this chapter, a teacher's role in several storymaking events was explored to gain insight into the nature of intertextuality. The perspective suggests that all authors' texts are read against the background of other authors' texts, and all storymaking events are read against the background of other storymaking events.

Intertextuality in the events in Vivian's classroom was evident on several levels. First, intertextuality occurred in the connections between the authors' texts across events. Second, intertextuality was evident in the ways of talking about authors' texts as reflected in the participants' discourse. Third, intertextuality was present in terms of the rules and expectations for participation in group processes. The analyses showed that observing multiple text events in classrooms can offer insights into the connections between authors' texts, ways of storymaking, and expectations for participation in group.

In exploring the nature of intertextuality, observe the intertextual links across authors' texts and storymaking events in a particular classroom.

- Consider the links between authors' texts.

  How are texts by the same author connected?
  How are texts in the same genre related?
  How are texts with similar themes linked?

- Consider the connections between storymaking events.

  What are the expectations for storymaking across events?
  What is the role of the teacher in different events?
  What is the role of the students in different events?
  Does the author's text influence the nature of the event?

- Consider the connections between group discussions.

  Are rules and expectations for participation evident across events?
  What is the function of the rules and expectations for facilitating storymaking processes?

# III

## ISSUES, DIRECTIONS, AND TEXTUAL PRACTICES

# 7

# Toward a Dialogue:
# Questions and Issues

In this chapter, the questions and issues discussed can provide a basis for dialogue and lead to action research and collaborative studies that explore the nature and function of texts in a variety of discourse events. The discussion of storymaking abilities focuses on the student and the storymaking abilities that are needed in developing communicative competence.

This inquiry has provided several insights into how narrative texts in classroom events are embedded in discourse processes governed by social expectations held by teachers and students.

- The contribution of each participant in the event influences the nature and significance of the story: the author's and illustrator's cues, the reader's cognitive and affective operations, and the student–teacher–text interactions both within and across classroom events.
- Certain characteristics of participants' contributions lend themselves to qualitatively different processes and outcomes than others. For example, adapted versions place different demands on the reader than original versions; the mode of the reactive text reveals different glimpses into the reader's tacit dimension; and the various ways teachers structure and mediate narrative events influence meaning-making processes.
- Certain authors' texts, readers' reactive texts, and teachers' styles of mediation may be more effective than others in preparing students for

successful encounters with narratives and for participation in the social construction of meanings.
• Some ways of looking at classroom events heighten our understanding
  concerning the nature of narrative text and how it is embedded in social discourse processes.

More importantly, however, the inquiry generates questions and issues
instead of providing answers or prescriptions.

## QUESTIONS AND ISSUES

Some questions regarding participants in storymaking processes were raised
either directly or indirectly in this exploration. To consider these questions
and issues, we first examine those related to the authors' texts and the individual reader's interactions with texts, the role of the participants in the discourse event, and the way their interactions influence the construction of
reactive texts.

### Authors' Texts

Several questions are pertinent to narrative texts; that is, those texts that
historically have evoked processes of narrativity. Which texts are selected?
Who has access to which texts? What functions do the texts serve?

In some classrooms, the texts chosen for focus are those typically associated with the literary canon. These texts are politicized in two ways. Often
the authors are from the dominant culture, which values their texts,
whereas other voices, such as those of women and ethnic writers, are
marginalized. When these valued narrative texts are used in the curriculum,
they perpetuate or reproduce the mainstream culture. Those who support
the use of texts from the canon argue that their value is related to their lon-
gevity and their ability to communicate "universal" values. Those who challenge the hegemony of these texts contend that mainstream works should
not be accorded the status of primary texts.

Not only are nonmainstream authors marginalized, but certain students
as well. In some instances, for example, only students in a particular "academic" track have access to these privileged texts. While this track of students experiences the "great books," the "nonacademic" or "general" track
students read other, perhaps less prestigious, texts (as determined by the system). In this way, the literary heritage approach perpetuates a class system
by valuing certain authors' texts over others and by limiting access of these
texts to certain groups of students.

In addition, access to texts is sometimes differentiated according to perceptions of reading ability level. Students identified as poor readers either work on skills in small groups or are removed from the classroom for special instruction, thereby missing out on the narrative texts experienced by their classmates. In Vivian's classroom, for example, certain students were removed from the reading-aloud event for special instruction, rejoining the whole group midway through the event. In this way, they missed the teacher's orientation to the event and the first part of the text. Furthermore, students in the lower track, many of them from nonmainstream cultures, experience a narrative event different from that of students in college prep tracks. Moreover, students designated as lower ability readers spend time working on the subskills associated with reading (Collins, 1986; McDermott, 1978). Standardized tests, which channel these students into particular groups, are based on the view that reading has its basis in what can be measured by a paper and pencil test.

Whereas some classrooms may emphasize "classics," others primarily use instructional texts designed specifically for particular grades or reading levels. In competing for school markets, publishing companies write texts that are graded to "readability" levels and that appease public interest groups in terms of controversial issues and language. Thus, instructional texts often represent doctored versions of original texts or excerpts from texts that will avoid controversy among community groups. Instructional texts and anthologies have their limitations. To capture a range of text types and to meet space requirements, basal readers and anthologies include texts that are perceived as representing different genres. Sometimes this results in the use of a token text to represent a certain type of text or narrative world as in the example of "multicultural" texts.

The excerpt from *Homesick*, for example, was a token multicultural work in that it was the only one in that basal series to relate the experiences of a character in a foreign country, and in that it was a slice of the character's broader experiences living in a different culture. Another issue is evident from this example. In the basal version the foreground experience of the character is that of a proud American. That is, the patriotic episode in the narrative is signaled in the words that frame the text, and several cultural references are deleted from the adapted text, resulting in a more pronounced focus on the character's patriotism. To some degree, the text is deculturalized and transformed into a more ethnocentric text, which reinforces the value of being an American.

Another concern about students experiencing predominantly instructional writings is that they will be exposed to texts they will not encounter in the world outside the classroom. These practice writings are designed to facilitate students' reading of particular kinds of texts such as excerpts, texts with controlled vocabulary, and texts that omit passages from the original, ostensibly to motivate the students to read the original, but perhaps also for financial reasons pertaining to limited space. Some research has shown that such alterations contribute to making the text more difficult to read, thereby inhibiting the development of textual strategies (Davison, 1984). For students whose experience is limited to exemplars from the literary canon, the range of texts also is narrowed considerably. By learning about specific texts, students may not acquire the strategies necessary for reading a variety of texts.

The preceding examples illustrate some of the issues related to the authors' texts that teachers select and make available to students. In some classrooms, however, students are free to select the works they want to read. This freedom may be designated by certain times set aside for reading, or in a more limited way, by time to read after other work is finished, although some students may never get to this point.

If student selection is the primary basis for reading, another potential source of problems can occur. Students may limit themselves to reading texts of certain authors, genres, and complexity levels. As a result, they may not experience narratives for the purpose of looking at self and the world in a new way, but may use literature only to reinforce the present self. This is evident when reader response journals of different students are considered. In contrast to Diane's journal entries discussed in chapter 5, Doug's responses during the same period reflected texts representing one genre, generally formulaic in nature, at a similar level of complexity. In her comments in the journal, Elaine encouraged Doug to read other books, but he remained fairly consistent in his choices and his way of responding throughout the year. If the reader response journal had been the sole basis of the literature program, this student would not have experienced a range of text types written by a variety of authors for different purposes. However, texts in Elaine's classroom included those she selected such as Paterson's (1977) *Bridge to Terabithia*, texts from a basal she was required to use, and texts students selected for their independent reading program.

## Texts in Discourse Events

A central question regarding the student reader asks which interpretations are acceptable and whose interpretations are legitimized. In an approach that allows only one acceptable interpretation of the text, the critic, the teacher, or the instructional program author may be the authority whose interpretation is sanctioned. This results in adherence to a meaning that reflects the bent of the particular interpreter. In one sense, the interpreter could foster a particular view of the world, as in a Marxist interpretation, and cause the narrative to be seen from this perspective. The text then is communicated to the student as a reflection of someone's perceived reality in the world. In some classrooms, the students' views are subordinate to these perspectives. Politically speaking, the student reader is reduced to a passive receiver rather than an active, critical interpreter. Such a role of passivity could create limited ways of engaging with texts outside the schooling experience. The reader may not learn to perceive of him- or herself as an active storymaker, but rather as a passive translator of an authoritative text such as a critic's text.

The consequences for the reader when others' interpretations are privileged is that the reader may find him- or herself subject to the tyranny of others' ideas, thereby negating self as an active meaning-maker. Consequently, readers may become tentative about offering their own interpretations because they have not experienced the text in terms of its multiple meanings. That is, they have not experienced the text as a dynamic force that grows and changes within the mind on subsequent readings and through interactions with other readers. By elevating some interpretations over others, we are sustaining an elite group of interpreters who have the final word in designating what a text means. This elite group may reflect current trends in literary criticism or certain political agendas. In the case of instructional programs, the instructional authors' interpretations may achieve status. This packaging of authors' texts and sanctioned interpretations legitimizes these interpreters to the point that their texts, rather than the classroom participants', are the object of study. This situation in which narrative texts are accompanied by critics' reactive texts seems to be a characteristic of schooling experiences rather than experiences outside the classroom.

At the other extreme, the practice of encouraging students to contribute any meaning can foster anarchy and relativity of interpretations. There is no responsibility or accountability to the author's or illustrator's text because meaning is whatever the individual reader decides it is. The authority of the individual reader can threaten the building of a social community of readers if the individual continually copies self instead of reinventing self through encounters with texts and other readers. Construction of meaning is always embedded to some degree in the social fabric of communities in which individual perceptions are open to modification, elaboration, confirmation, and challenge through discourse processes. The tyranny of an individual breaks up the potential connections between the author's text and the community of interpreters.

Another issue relevant in discourse events is the function that literature serves. Texts are used for a variety of purposes, including their use as a vehicle for teaching skills, as an object for literary analysis, as a conveyor of values, as a means of entertainment, and as an experience of aesthetic dimensions. If any one function is dominant or used to the exclusion of others, the reader will not experience the full potential of literature.

Furthermore, certain functions, when considered in classroom contexts, are controversial, such as the view that the purpose of literature is to create an awareness of values. Yet, is the purpose of literature to teach values? If so, what and whose values should be taught? This issue is highlighted when conflicts arise between the teacher and members of the local community, as witnessed in numerous censorship cases. The value of tolerance toward those who are different, for example, may be valued in the classroom yet challenged by some community members. Furthermore, some community members may oppose the concept of teaching values in classrooms, viewing this as a parental responsibility. In addition, a value promoted through a particular text can be interpreted differently by opposing groups. One group may see the picture book *Sadako* describing the death of a Japanese girl from the radiation effects after the bombing of Hiroshima as valuing peace, whereas another may view it as encouraging antiwar or anti-American sentiment.

## A PERSPECTIVE ON STORYMAKING ABILITIES

What constitutes abilities in storymaking? We begin addressing this question with a conception of what constitutes communicative competence. From a sociolinguistic perspective, communicative competence entails the ability to produce and comprehend a range of discourses in a variety of contexts for different purposes (Hymes, 1974). Building on this conception, narrative competence involves the ability to construct and signify a range of authors' texts in a variety of contexts for different purposes. Inherent in this view of storymaking ability is the notion that successful story construction and interpretation involves a complex interaction of linguistic, social, and cognitive factors, underscoring its pragmatic nature.

To explore abilities in storymaking more fully, we can focus on three indications of communicative competence noted earlier.

### Construct and Interpret a Range of Stories

One way to explore this ability is to consider the implied reader that lays down the role in the text for the actual reader. Theoretically, this implied reader is expected to take up activities related to constructing, interpreting, and signifying narrative texts, such as translating and integrating information and filling in the unwritten parts of the narrative. To experience successfully a range of narratives, the reader must assume the following additional roles indicated by the implied reader for different genres:

- Suspend disbelief when entering the fantasy world.
- Assemble clues and anticipate solutions in reading mysteries.
- Empathize and/or identify with characters who have problems in contemporary realism.
- See another's perspective in reading about characters from different cultures.
- Speculate about the consequences of scientific advances in science fiction.
- Find humor in ridiculous situations with preposterous characters.
- Vicariously experience survival adventures.

Competence therefore involves the ability to take on the general role of readers of all narratives as well as to assume the role of the implied reader for specific narratives. In the latter case, the reader demonstrates an ability to adjust to the demands of the varying textual guides and expectations for the reader's performance.

Also related to the ability to engage in a range of narrative texts is the reader's ability to adjust to the demands of the narrative in different modes. Narratives appear in many forms or agencies, and the interpreter must be able to recognize and use the textual guides appearing along different continua in these channels. For example, when the interpreter encounters a narrative in picture book form, it is often in a read-aloud process, so the interpreter must be able to sort out the textual guides in the author's words, the illustrator's pictures, and the reader's rendering. Because picture books vary in the ways that words and pictures interrelate, the interpreter must be able to adjust to different patterns. In some books, for example, words are predominant and pictures illustrate a small segment of the text on a given page. In other books, words and pictures carry the same information. In still others, the pictures carry the primary information, and the words function as captions (Golden, 1990). Some picture books require the interpreter to follow both a visual and a textual storyline that may not be synonymous, as exemplified in Hutchins' (1968) *Rosie's Walk* and Raskins' (1966) *Nothing Ever Happens on My Block*, in which the words tell one character's perspective and the pictures tell that of another.

In storytelling events, the conveyer of the tale serves as an interpreter who relays the narrative through words as well as paralinguistic and kinesic cues. In some events, the reader is required to assume an active role as an audience who responds and participates in the performance of the story. The interpreter in this case takes on the general role of reader, the specific role of interpreter of genres such as folktales, and the role of the audience who listens and participates in the event.

In responding to film, the interpreter constructs the narrative guided by conversations and actions of characters who enact and react to events. In some cases, a voice-over narrator is present, whereas in many cases there is no narrator. Interpreters perceive a linear flow of visual images. Like written genres, film genres evoke different levels of participation, such as the vicarious adventure experience or a cultural experience different from one's own (Golden, 1990).

## Construct and Interpret Texts in Different Contexts

Because children's storymaking is essentially a social process, they experience it in different contexts including home, school, and community. These situations may involve an adult mediating the experience. The process of register switching can be seen in children's ability to adjust to the social demands of different contexts. In a home setting, for example, the child may encounter narratives in a variety of structured and unstructured ways with different family members and friends. These narratives may appear in various channels that place different demands on the interpreter such as book reading events, television narratives, and film narratives. Explicit expectations of adults about the way to make meaning in these events may or may not be formalized.

When children encounter narratives in community settings, other expectations for meaning may be present. In some communities, for example, narratives are conveyed through storytelling accompanied by expectations for the way audiences are to participate. In library story hours, rules for the reading-aloud event are established, and children must adjust to these expectations.

Classrooms pose another set of expectations about the way to enter and participate in storymaking. These expectations can shift across events in the same classroom, as when students participate in a storybook reading event, when they read silently, and when they write responses in their journals. Students also must adjust to the social negotiation of meaning present in classrooms wherein their individual interpretations are open to modification, challenge, confirmation, and elaboration by other participants. Thus, there are academic ways of meaning that vary within and across classrooms as well as home and community ways of meaning. Ways of "doing" narrative in one context may either be compatible or clash with those in another.

There is a concern that a reader judged to be competent in a classroom setting may be the one who learns or already possesses the skills valued in that particular environment. In other words, each child may demonstrate storymaking competence in home and community contexts, but not be perceived as competent in the classroom context. By recognizing multiple competencies in different contexts, teachers can build on one kind of capability and extend it to capabilities in other contexts. By not acknowledging multiple narrative competencies, educators limit the notion of what constitutes storymaking capabilities in different contexts. Concomitantly, students with mainstream ways of meaning that may more directly match academic ways of meaning are, in turn, limited by a narrow interpretation of meaning-making. Students should be exposed to storymaking expectations in a variety of contexts so they experience the social roots of making meaning.

### Engage With Authors' Texts for a Variety of Purposes

A primary purpose associated with fictional narratives is to experience their poetic or aesthetic dimensions. As Rosenblatt (1976) argued, readers should be able to participate in a "lived-through experience" as they construct and interpret the text during the reading process. This experience, at some point and with some texts, should lead to the narrative signifying something for the reader, that is, creating an effect on the reader that will enable him or her to look at self and the world in a new way (Iser, 1978). Thus, the aesthetic function as it pertains to the "lived-through experience" is always central in the construction and interpretation of narratives.

Other purposes are also evident. The "lived-through experience" of a secondary world does not always lead to a reconceptualization of self and the world. Texts can be read for purposes of amusement or entertainment, emphasizing the vicarious experience of the reader. Involvement with such texts can end after the book is read, as in the case of some mysteries and stories with preposterous characters (although who can say which stories live on in the minds of readers). Other texts may be read for the purpose of understanding another's perspective, such as historical fiction that relates events experienced by characters in crises. Both the genre and the reader's personal reasons for reading work together to influence the purpose of storymaking processes.

In school settings, readers may be asked to read for a variety of purposes, some of which are consistent with their typical reasons for reading, and some of which are not. Readers in classroom settings, for example, may be asked to read a text for instructional ends that they normally would read for entertainment purposes. Setting the purpose for reading will influence how they construct, interpret, and signify the text in the classroom setting.

In the Pecos Bill event, Annyce set the purpose for reading the text: to see how the truth was stretched. She wanted her students to understand the tall tale genre and write stories about the character. The students purposes may have been to read the story for entertainment reasons. Success in school is determined by students' ability to construct narratives for different purposes.

## A LOOK AT NONFICTION NARRATIVES

The emphasis of the present volume has been on the exploration of fictional narratives. It is important to consider other kinds of narratives as well because narrative is a primary way of organizing experience, knowledge, and imagination. Some of these narrative types are discussed in the following sections.

### Narrative Poems

Narrative poems, similar to fictional prose, engage the interpreter in constructing, interpreting, and signifying narrative worlds for aesthetic purposes. The interpreter is guided by textual cues indicating character, time, and narrative focalization. In contrast to a prose narrative, the textual information in a poem is arranged in verse form, which may influence how the reader constructs the narrative. Some narrative poems, like fictional narratives, can relate stories of actual events and time relations among events, such as "The Charge of the Light Brigade," and stories about actual persons such as "Paul Revere's Ride." Fictional characters and events such as Little Orphan Annie or personified animals such as the Owl and the Pussycat also are featured in narrative poems. In narrative poems, ballads, epics, limericks, and some nursery rhymes, characters enact and react to events filtered through the lens of a narrator.

### Personal Narratives

Personal narratives appear in everyday life as a way of representing experiences and expressing self. In conversations, a speaker conveys a sequence of events to a listener to provide information, among other purposes. Depending on the relationship between the speaker and the listener, the listener is invited to take up various roles in response to the narrative (e.g., acknowledgment, advice). Personal narratives also are evident in dialogue journals where students recount their experiences in sharing time, during which students tell about episodes in their lives, or in discussions that afford students the opportunity to tie in their personal experiences.

How individuals represent their personal narratives reflects individual differences as well as cultural ways of organizing experiences. According to Michaels (1981), some students use associative chains, whereas others use topic chains. The latter are more like school-based ways of representing experiences. Thus, there are different ways of narrating personal experiences. Furthermore, the notion of what is a "true" story versus an imaginative story reflects both individual and cultural ways of communicating personal stories, which should be taken into account. Classroom participants must learn to shift stances to allow for different ways of representing meaning.

## Rhetorical Narratives

Rhetorical narratives are embedded in other types of discourse, serving as both information and rhetorical examples. Stories, either apocryphal or true, are used in sermons for rhetorical purposes or to clarify concepts or illustrate concepts (e.g., parables, allegories). In political speeches, narratives are used to illustrate a particular political perspective, such as the recounting of the story about a real hero who exemplifies a value. Narratives are used rhetorically in advertisements to persuade individuals to buy a product, contribute to a cause, or join a campaign.

The audience for such discourse has to participate in constructing and interpreting events, connecting the narrative example to the discourse in which it is embedded and establishing the significance of the narrative, which may concur or contrast with the speaker's sense of the significance. Essentially, the interpreter must be aware that narrative is used for rhetorical purposes. Therefore, he or she must actively make a choice as to whether the example is persuasive.

## News Event Narratives

Informational narrative is used to convey ongoing reports of current events as in on-the-scene news reporting, sportcasting or interpretating of news, sports, and other events after they have occurred. Interpretation of events by the audience requires the construction of events and an awareness that events are a part of a wider pattern of events, that news reporters mediate events, that news is filtered through a lens, and that news reporters often disclose which events they perceive as significant. Thus, the interpreter not only has to construct the narrative world, but also must signify that world by attending to different perspectives. The interpreter moves between different channels such as newspapers and television, and across multiple perspectives such as conservative, liberal, and so forth.

## Historical Narratives

Historical narratives provide an interesting comparison with fictional narratives. Historical texts, like literary narratives and the other narratives discussed earlier, are potential signs to be constructed, interpreted, and signified. Although there may be higher intersubjective agreement about the events that transpired during a certain period (although this might be open to debate), the events are not viewed in terms of themselves, but in relation to a set of facts existing in other accounts. Thus, facts are assumed when multiple accounts of events reflect the same individuals and sequence of events. There can be discrepancy, however, in which events are emphasized in certain accounts. Some texts, such as *Underside of American History and Other Readings* (Frazier, 1971), were written to present a perspective on the history of women and minority groups largely neglected in accounts of history emphasizing contributions and perspectives of White males.

The way events and individuals are interpreted also illustrates the parallel between historical texts and fictional narrative texts. Both are polysemous in nature in that more than one interpretation of events is possible (e.g., a social interpretation, a Marxist interpretation, a revisionist interpretation). Very different pictures emerge of "Manifest Destiny" depending on the perspective of the historian. In one account, it is conveyed from a patriotic slant on the westward expansion of America. In another account, it is portrayed as fostering a policy of genocide.

## Biographies

Biographies are another form of narrative. The purpose for reading biography is to learn about an individual's life and times. Like historical accounts, biographies also reflect varied interpretations of particular figures. Some historians begin with a theme about the individual's life and organize information within that framework, whereas the interpretations of others are guided by the direction indicated by the "facts." In books written for child audiences, biography is termed as "authentic" or "fictionalized" (Huck, Heplar, Hickman & Kiefer, 1997). In "authentic" biography, the author reports only what is verified from primary sources, whereas in fictional biography, the author takes liberties, not with facts, but in using invented dialogues and scenes for narrative purposes. Even in authentic biographies for children, however, the secondary sources the author drew on in writing the biography are not necessarily included.

One issue concerning the notion of authentic is that it implies an authoritative account of an individual's life. Clearly, historical accounts vary widely depending on which facts the author selects, and how the facts are arranged and interpreted. Therefore, reading several different "authentic" biographies of Christopher Columbus or George Custer, for example, can lead to very different portraits of these individuals. They may be portrayed as heroic in one biography, villainous in another, or in terms of strengths and weaknesses in still another biography. To present a biography as nonfiction, on one level, suggests to students that biography represents a compendium of "true" facts divorced from an interpretive process involving both the author and the reader. Even though "verified" facts are employed in a narrative, there is still a narrator who conveys the story of an individual from a particular perspective, who focalizes the individual and the events. The reader of a biography, then, performs the same cognitive operations in constructing other narratives, with the added recognition that formulating a fuller view of an individual requires interpreting more than one biography (as well as other types of accounts) about that individual.

### Scientific Narratives

Science concepts also are presented through narrative texts such as reports of experiments, descriptions of animals' life cycles or a day in the life of an animal, and accounts of how the earth was formed. Again, there are established "facts" regarding certain scientific phenomena, such as how babies are born, which are agreed on and perhaps not open to a variety of interpretations. Lemke (1995) discussed constructing meaning from a social semiotic perspective to illustrate how students learn to establish semantic networks of concepts in a social interactive process with other class participants. In science, some "facts" are open to multiple interpretations, such as how the world was created. In other areas, answers are not known, and students are invited to formulate their own speculations through narrative and other discourse forms.

Some individuals, in contrast to traditional concepts of science, view it as a basis for a meaning construction process in which "readers" are guided by cues in the data. Thus, the potential sign is transformed into a scientific premise, which signifies in various ways to different students. Here, text is viewed in its broadest possible sense as a potential phenomena that appears in many forms, including observed events, demonstrations, scenes, or reported events in texts, as well as in teacher's discourse (e.g., lectures).

## Game Narratives

Narratives also appear in children's games such those based on nursery rhymes ("London Bridge is Falling Down"), play situations with dolls and other objects, dungeons and dragons, real-life play situations such as that of doctor and super heroes, puppet shows, and so forth. Narratives appear in riddles, puzzles, and joke formats, with characters enacting events and reacting to them. Narratives appear in entertainment programs for children as well as instructional programs, and in cartoons.

The preceding examples of narratives illustrate both common and divergent aspects of storymaking processes. These types share the common characteristics of relating actions performed and reacted to by agents in a time and space conveyed by a narrator. These narratives require readers to construct, interpret, and signify the narrative text, observing both textual and contextual cues. The interpreter translates and combines textual information, fills in the unwritten or unspoken parts of the narrative, and integrates information into narrative patterns of characters, events, and narrator.

The different types of narrative texts, however, also place different demands on the reader according to the type of narrative, the channel, the function, and the context in which it appears. Storymaking ability involves the students' strategies for engaging in the process of narrativity pertaining to a range of narrative texts in a variety of contexts for different purposes.

The discussion suggests several implications for the development of storymaking abilities in classroom settings. In selecting texts, the teacher must recognize the variety of narrative texts and the demands they place on the reader. Students should have the opportunity to experience a range of authors, genres, cultures, and modes.

The teacher also must recognize the problematic aspects of viewing any work as "authoritative," including so-called nonfictional texts. The constructive and interpretive involvement of the reader is central in any interaction between readers and texts. Unlike fictional narratives, informational narratives may represent a place along the continuum of texts at which "facts" can be confirmed by referring to texts outside the text. In addition, students should actively participate in establishing the significance of narrative rather than merely subscribing to what a literary critic determines to be important.

## BRIDGING THEORY INTO PRACTICE

The questions and issues raised in this chapter offer a starting point for examining the specific authors' texts selected for storymaking events and how students have access to the texts. Related to this issue is the function that literature serves in the classroom, such as introducing students to certain texts, developing values, and motivating reader response, among others.

The chapter also suggests the need to look at how the authors' texts are constructed and interpreted in classroom events, and how reactive texts of teachers, critics, instructional program authors, and students are valued. By addressing these issues, it is possible to examine more closely the reasons for choosing particular texts, connecting particular texts with certain readers, and valuing certain constructions and interpretations over others.

To explore these questions and issues, observe a particular classroom to determine the authors' texts in use, students' access to the texts, and how students' reactive texts are assessed.

- Consider which texts are in use.

  Are certain authors' texts valued?
  Do all students have the same access to the same texts?

- Consider the expectations for reactive texts.

  Are certain types of reactive texts valued over others?
  Do all students produce the same reactive texts?
  How are reactive texts assessed?
  What is the weight of the teacher's, critics', and instructional program authors' reactive texts?

- Consider the function that texts serve.

  What are the purposes for using authors' texts?
  Is there a dominant function that the authors' texts serve?

# 8

# Developing Storymaking Abilities in Classrooms

In this chapter, the ways in which authors' texts and teachers' approaches can contribute to the development of students' storymaking abilities are addressed. Considerations pertaining to selecting a range of authors' texts are outlined. Specific ways in which teachers can support students' interaction with authors' texts are noted. The contributions of the author's text, the teacher, and the students are also represented.

As discussed previously, a major function of schools is to develop students' abilities as sign-makers by guiding their learning of how to construct, interpret, and signify a range of authors' texts in a variety of situations for different purposes. As complex semiotic systems, classrooms can offer opportunities for students to engage actively in storymaking processes and to reflect on the ways in which textual meaning is socially constructed through discourse. Both the authors' texts and the teacher's ways of storymaking influence how the students develop their textual abilities.

## AUTHORS' TEXTS

Central to storymaking processes is the readers' ability to identify a text as a narrative and to invoke the expectations pertaining to narrative structures and conventions. When readers encounter narrative texts, they anticipate that a narrator will convey a sequence of events enacted and reacted to by characters in time and space. Characters can be revealed through their actions, speech, thoughts, other characters' views, and the narrator. Time re-lations will be established through various cues that indicate how frequent, how long, and in what order events occur. They will find a narrator outside the events or as a character also in the story, which will be filtered from the perspective of one character or that of many characters. Skilled readers also know how narrative elements appear in different texts influenced by the style of the author, the genre of the narrative text, and the channel in which the text is transmitted.

Students can develop an awareness of how to construct and interpret narrative texts in general and how to read particular narrative texts when they have opportunities in the classroom to experience many different narrative texts.

## A Range of Voices

Texts should reflect the voices of many authors, including authors from different cultural groups in the United States and authors from different cultures elsewhere. A single voice should not be used as representative of a particular ethnic group. The African American author Virginia Hamilton has written narrative texts representing a range of genres as well as those that blur genre lines. Her African American characters live in such settings as urban ghettos, Appalachian Mountain communities, and small middle-class towns. Her characters reflect a range of voices speaking of their challenge to find their identities and seeking strength in the histories of their people. Her texts reflect contemporary realism, fantasy, and a collection of African American folklore.

Other African American authors include Sharon Bell Mathis, Walter Dean Myers, Eloise Greenfield, Lucille Clifton, and Mildred Taylor. Together, these and other authors' books represent a range of styles, tones, and perspectives on the experiences of African American characters. Jean Fritz's *Homesick* shows one Westerner's view of living in China as the hostility of the Chinese against foreigners mounted in the early 20th century. Lawrence Yep in *Serpent's Children* relates the story of a Chinese character caught in the conflict against Manchu and British rule in 19th century China, which approaches the antagonism toward foreigners from a Chinese character's perspective. Another story by Yep, *Child of the Owl*, focuses on a Chinese American character searching for her roots.

In terms of folktales, multicultural sources are needed, not limiting students' experiences to the European traditions expressed in the tales by the Grimms and Perrault. Tales from a variety of cultures including those from India, Nigeria, Mexico, Egypt, and Brazil, among many other countries, are needed to provide a spectrum of folklore texts.

Several issues arise in relation to grouping texts into "cultural" units. A major issue concerns the grouping of Native Americans together without differentiating tribes. A second issue pertains to placing narratives associated with one cultural group together in a unit, such as Native American literature. The implication is that this is a different, and perhaps less valuable, type of literature because it is not woven throughout the curriculum. A third issue is that any juxtaposition of texts reflects the teacher's view of thematic connections instead of allowing for a student's formulation of themes and discovery of intertextual connections among narratives from similar and different cultures.

## A Range of Genres

In addition to texts reflecting a range of author's voices, works also should represent a range of genres with several rather than single texts from different genres. Because the notion of genre itself is a controversial way of designating texts, the complexities of works within each genre should be explored. On one level, there is no ideal folktale schema reflected in folktales. Different types of tales exist within and across cultures including trickster tales, pourquoi tales, fairy tales, and so forth. Different cultural groups have contrastive ways of narrating stories, which may include associative chains of events as opposed to linear arrangements. One way of representing events is not superior to another. Folktales and myths are echoed in modern hero fantasy. Readers familiar with conventions of hero myths and folktales will recognize similar conventions in high fantasy set in secondary worlds with heroes guided by powerful mentors as they fight evil forces. In reading a second and third book in a sequel or a series of chronicles, readers can build on previous texts to enrich the continuing tales of heroes. Similarly, modern fairy tales and fables have their roots in the oral tradition. Children can find connections between the modern fables of Lionni and Lobel, for example, and fables from the oral tradition in various cultures.

In contrast to fantasy, readers can experience connections to characters in real-life settings, both past and present, through contemporary and historical fiction. This literature provides a basis for readers to find themselves reflected in the plausible world of a character or to discover other's experiences in realistic worlds outside their own experiences. Realistic texts are not always serious in tone, but also reflect stories with humorous tones such as Rockwell's *How to Eat Fried Worms*. By learning to read a variety of genres, students develop skills in adjusting to the different demands of literature and the different purposes for reading literature such as reading for amusement, social understanding, or personal identification.

## A Range of Channels

To build sign capability within and across channels, students should have the opportunity to engage in and develop strategies for experiencing narratives in a variety of ways. As noted previously, picture books constitute a complex array of texts in which word and picture clues are connected in different ways. A number of aspects associated with these relationships can be experienced, including texts in which pictures and words generally communicate similar information, texts in which words carry the primary information and pictures emphasize aspects of the text, texts in which pictures carry primary information and words serve as captions, and texts in which pictures enhance the story through the use of visual elements.

Accompanying these considerations are those pertaining to the range of authors and illustrators and their artistic style (e.g., expressionistic) and their use of visual elements (e.g., line, color). Other formats for presenting narratives in written form include chapter books (e.g., *Bridge to Terabithia*), illustrated narratives (e.g., *The Hundred Penny Box*), and independent readers (e.g., *Frog and Toad*). Other narratives appear in film form as a display of moving images of actions and scenes accompanied by characters' dialogues. Students can explore what happens to a narrative originally appearing in written form when it is adapted to a film medium, for example, comparing Hans Christian Andersen's *The Little Mermaid* with the Disney studio's adaptation. In addition to experiencing written and film narratives, students can experience stories orally during storytelling performances, thus engaging in a communal experience with text that involves their participation in a different kind of way.

## A Range in Complexity

A range in complexity suggests the need to challenge traditional concepts of "readability." First, we can challenge the notion, based on some studies, that writing or rewriting a text to make it conform to a particular reading level results in making it more accessible to readers.

Factors other than those considered in these formulas must be taken into account. Within any given classroom, a range of reading levels exists, so why should texts conform to a particular level?

A variety of factors contributes to a text's complexity. Texts with figurative and symbolic language, for example, are more challenging to read than those that reflect literal language. Texts with challenging vocabulary are more difficult than texts with easier vocabulary (e.g., Steig's descriptions in *Amos and Boris*). Texts that involve the reader in drawing inferences about the character's traits, such as Hamilton's *Sweet Whispers, Brother Rush*, are more complex than those such as Lindgren's *Pippi Longstocking*, in which the narrator describes the character.

Texts that require a background knowledge of conventions, such as LeGuin's high fantasy trilogy of *Earthsea*, are more difficult to read than some humorous fantasies, such as *Paddington*. Texts also may differ in complexity of the topics they address, as is evident in contemporary realism. For example, topics concerning a character's conflict with substance abuse or growing awareness of sexuality are more difficult for younger readers who may not have the background knowledge, experience, or interest to construct and interpret such narratives. Thus, within a given classroom, narrative texts should reflect a range of complexity levels that take into account the author's language, the topic, the demands of the genre, the format of the book (e.g., picture books, illustrated narratives), and factors associated with the reader.

## THE TEACHER AS FACILITATOR

In classroom settings, narrative texts are embedded in a social discourse between teachers and students. Although teacher and students co-construct the storymaking event, the teacher plays a pivotal role in orchestrating the process. Students hold expectations, not only about the narrative text, but also about the nature of the event—its structure and conventions of discourse. Events will be conducted according to social rules for participation such as turn-taking and listening to other participants. Academic rules consider the ways that texts are socially constructed and interpreted, how channel cues are signaled, and how texts are linked to other texts.

Teachers can facilitate students' storymaking abilities by allowing for different ways of selecting texts, providing equal access to texts, varying scaffolding strategies, using a variety of channels, employing a range of assessments, using texts for different purposes, and embedding texts in different contexts.

### Allowing for Teacher and Student Selections

Texts incorporated into classroom-related processes should represent both teacher-selected and student-selected works. Teachers may seek to select a range of texts to expose their students to different kinds of literature, different authors, different complexity levels, and so forth. Teachers also may select books to highlight certain themes or literary elements and to use narrative works across the curriculum. To accomplish instructional goals, then, the way the teacher selects texts can play a critical role in the development of students' sign competence. A good method of selection will ensure that students will read a range of texts and discover intertextual relations among texts.

Students also should have the opportunity to select their own texts. In doing so, they can set their own purposes for reading and have the opportunity to read what interests them. Their role in selection may motivate them to read outside the classroom during and after their schooling experiences.

## Providing for Access to Texts

This aspect suggests that students should have opportunities to engage with texts. Rather than encountering a text to merely learn a skill or concept, reading a book if they finish their work, or listening to books read aloud as a transitional activity, students should have sustained times for reading literature that are built into the classroom day. Furthermore, all students, no matter what their perceived level of reading ability, should have equal access to texts.

## Varying Scaffolding Strategies

Mediated events in which students interact with teachers should reflect a variety of structures and uses of language. Formulaic scaffolding in which the teacher always begins with a prediction question, that observes a question–answer format during the reading of the text, and that ends with follow-up questions is not the only type of structure and mediation. In structuring events, teachers might read aloud and respond to student-generated observations. Teachers can offer statements rather than questions when they participate in discussions. Sharing of a book can, at times, occur without accompanying teacher talk, reading literature for an uninterrupted aesthetic experience.

## Encouraging a Variety of Channels for Reactive Texts

A variety of ways that encourage students' construction, interpretation, and signification of literature texts should be included in the classroom. This variety is needed for at least three reasons. First, because reactive texts present only glimpses of the tacit dimension, and because certain types of reactive texts elicit certain aspects of the reader's meaning (e.g., retellings versus journals), it is necessary to have various ways of responding to get a more comprehensive picture of children's storymaking abilities. Second, a variety of channels, including those elected on occasion by the students (i.e., letting the students choose the channel they want to use), enables students to develop a range of representational skills. They can learn to articulate their thoughts and ideas through drama, art, writing, and so forth. Third, a variety of reactive texts enables students to express texts individually (as in a journal) and also to work with other participants to express interpretations (as in a drama or discussion). This allows for the incorporation of private and public responses as well as the intersection between private and public responses (e.g., private readings as well as small group discussions).

## Using a Range of Assessments

Assessments of students' storymaking should be based on a range of reactive texts. Informal observations and checklists of the kinds of storymaking in which children are engaged will provide information on how they are expressing narrative texts. Independent reading programs can be monitored through responses to students' journals and book conferences can be conducted with students. Assessing students' abilities to use specific strategies related to the use of cues on the text continuum, applying prior knowledge, finding connections between texts, and developing abilities to express reactive texts (e.g., writing interpretations of characters) can be governed by the recognition that there is intersubject agreement on some aspects of text (e.g., events that occurred), and possible text variation in others (e.g., the character's motivation). No single assessment, such as answering questions at the end of the reading, and no single judgment of those answers (e.g., right vs. wrong interpretation) does justice to the complexity of the storymaking process.

## Ensuring a Choice of Different Purposes for Reading

The teacher should keep at the center of narrative storymaking the aesthetic function of the text. Narrative events should emphasize the "lived-through experience" with the text. To achieve this experience, the student has to develop skills in constructing, interpreting, and signifying narrative as he or she transforms the potential sign into an actual sign. Students should be given the opportunity to set their own purposes for reading, that is, to identify with a character, to read a book for entertainment purposes, or to experience a book recommended by a peer.

Teachers also can select books to highlight concepts—a book about rain on a rainy day, a book on working out conflict with peers, a book dealing with the death of a pet, or a book about characters from different cultural backgrounds. In using these texts, the students' interpretation and establishment of significance remains at the center of the experience.

On occasion, and with the recognition that the aesthetic experience is foremost, a book can be used to teach a particular reading skill such as predicting and problem solving in reading a mystery (e.g., Raskins' *The Westing Game*), combining factual information with fiction in reading a work of historical fiction (e.g., Lowry's *Number the Stars*), or recognizing that any given biography represents one perspective on a person's life (e.g., Colver's and Freedman's biographies of Lincoln).

## Embedding Texts in Contexts

A balance of embedding similar texts or noting parallels between texts will help students to establish intertextual links. Furthermore, this may help them in drawing on one text type to construct, interpret, and signify another as in the case of discovering connections between heroes in folklore and those in high fantasy. Texts may be arranged in units to highlight the teacher's conception of topic links (books on animals), books with similar settings (characters in World War II), books with similar themes (survival stories), books with the same character (e.g., biographies of Harriet Tubman), books of the same genre (e.g., pourquoi tales), books by the same author and illustrator (e.g., Maurice Sendak), and so forth.

Students also can be encouraged to discover their own sense of links between books that are not arranged in a unit. The teacher's arrangement of texts, to some degree, classifies texts as something, presupposing the teacher's construction, interpretation, and signification of texts. Therefore, students also must have the opportunity to read texts without connecting them to other texts and to make their own connections.

Texts are linked not only to other texts, but also to various subject areas. When texts are used across the curriculum, they can appear in association with topics of science, history, geography, health, and math. In relation to history, for example, exploration of the American Revolutionary period can include historical fiction such as *Johnny Tremain* and *My Brother Sam is Dead*. Books also can be embedded in the direct experiences of the students both inside and outside the classroom. A field trip to the shore, for example, can be accompanied by a reading of Garelick's *Down to the Beach*.

The contributions of the text, the student, and the teacher in the development of students' storymaking abilities is represented in Fig. 8.1. By specifying these contributions, we can identify how students can experience a range of texts in a variety of contexts for different purposes. Rather than to serve as a fixed, static model, this perspective on developing storymaking abilities is intended to invite readers to explore the ways in which teachers, students, and texts participate and interact in classroom settings. Many nar-

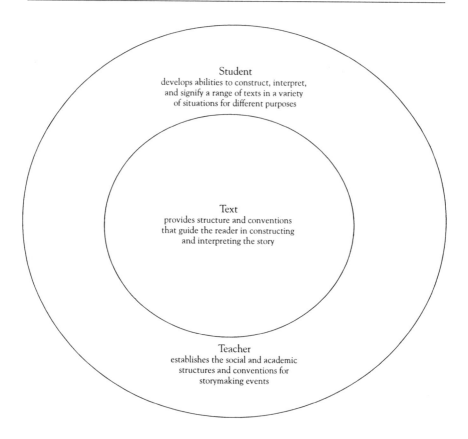

FIG. 8.1. Developing storymaking abilities in the classroom.

rative events must come into play as we discuss and refine our concepts of the nature and development of sign-making abilities.

## BRIDGING THEORY INTO PRACTICE

The social semiotic perspective applied in this chapter suggests that storymaking involves the ability to construct, interpret, and signify a range of narrative texts in a variety of contexts for different purposes. To support the development of a repertoire of strategies, students should encounter texts that represent a range of authors, genres, modes, and levels of complexity. The teacher can facilitate the development of storymaking abilities by allowing for teacher- and student-selected texts, creating opportunities for reading, using a variety of scaffolding approaches, including different types of reactive texts, using a range of means for assessing responses, and encouraging different purposes for storymaking.

To explore kinds of authors' texts and the role of the teacher as facilitator in storymaking events, study the role of the teacher and the texts in a particular classroom.

- Consider the kinds of authors' texts in the classroom.

  Which authors are included?
  What genres are represented?
  What channels are evident?
  Is there a range in complexity?

- Consider the role of the teacher as facilitator in the storymaking event.

  How are authors' texts selected?
  Do all students have access to the same texts?
  Are different ways of structuring events evident?
  How are different reactive texts assessed?
  What different purposes do the texts serve?
  How are texts used in different situations?

# References

Bakhtin, M. (1986). *Speech genres and other late essays* (V. W. McGee, Trans.). Austin: University of Texas Press.

Barthes, R. (1977). *Image music text* (S. Heath, Trans.). New York: Hill & Wang.

Barthes, R. (1979). From work to text. In J. V. Harari (Ed.), *Textual strategies: Perspectives in poststructuralist criticism* (pp. 73–81). Ithaca, NY: Cornell University Press.

Barton, D. (1994). *Literacy: An introduction to the ecology of written language.* Oxford, UK: Blackwell.

Bauman, R. (1986). *Story performance and event: Contextual studies in oral narrative.* Cambridge, UK: Cambridge University Press.

Beach, R., & Hynds, S. (1990). Research on response to literature. In R. Barr, M. Kamil, P. Mosenthal, & P. D. Pearson (Eds.), *Handbook of reading research* (Vol. 2, pp. 453–489). White Plains, NY: Longman.

Bloome, D. (1987). Reading as a social process in a middle school classroom. In D. Bloome (Ed.), *Literacy and schooling* (pp. 123–149). Norwood, NJ: Ablex.

Bloome, D., & Egan-Robertson, A. (1993). The social construction of intertextuality in classroom reading and writing lessons. *Reading Research Quarterly, 28,* 304–333.

Campbell, J. (1949). *The hero with a thousand faces.* Princeton, NJ: Princeton University Press.

Chatman, S. (1978). *Story and discourse: Narrative structure in fiction and film.* Ithaca, NY: Cornell University Press.

Cochran-Smith, M. (1984). *The making of a reader.* Norwood, NJ: Ablex.

Collins, J. (1986). Differential instruction reading groups. In J. Cook-Gumperz (Ed.), *The social construction of literacy* (pp. 117–137). Cambridge, UK: Cambridge University Press.

Cook-Gumperz, J. (1986). *The social construction of literacy.* Cambridge, UK: Cambridge University Press.

Dahl, R. (1974). The wish. In A. A. Kitzhaber (Gen. Ed.), *Patterns in literature* (pp. 279–281). New York: Holt, Rinehart & Winston.

Davis, K., & Golden, J. M. (1993, April). *Exploring culturally responsive pedagogy in a first-grade classroom.* Paper presented at the American Educational Research Association, San Francisco, CA.

Davis, K., & Golden, J. M. (1994). Teacher culture and student voices in an urban kindergarten center, *Linguistics and Education, 6*(3), 261–288.

Davison, A. (1984). Readability formulas and comprehension. In G. Duffy, L. Rohler, & J. Mason (Eds.), *Comprehension and instruction: Perspectives and suggestions* (pp. 128–143). New York: Longman.

de Beaugrande, R. (1980). *Text, discourse, and process: Toward a multidisciplinary science of texts.* Norwood, NJ: Ablex.

Fairclough, N. (1992). *Discourse and social change.* Cambridge, UK: Polity Press.

Fairclough, N. (1995). *Critical discourse analysis: The critical study of language.* London, UK: Longman.

Fish, S. (1980). *Is there a text in this classroom?* Cambridge, MA: Harvard University Press.

Fowler, R. (1996). *Linguistic criticism* (2nd ed.). Oxford, UK: Oxford University Press.

Fox, P. (1967). *How many miles to Babylon?* New York: Scholastic Book Services.

Frazier, T. R. (1971). (comp). *Underside of American History and other readings.* New York: Harcourt Brace Jovanovich.

Freeman, D. (1978). *A pocket for Corduroy.* New York: Viking.

Fritz, J. (1982). *Homesick.* New York: Dell.

Fritz, J. (1987). Homesick. In M. Early (Ed.), *Portraits* (pp. 306–321). New York: Harcourt Brace Jovanovich.

Galarza, E. (1978). Excerpt from barrio boy. In R. Ruddell, S. Sebesta, & E. J. Ahern (Eds.), *The widening path* (pp. 170–180). Boston, MA: Allyn & Bacon.

Genette, G. (1980). *Narrative discourse: An essay in method* (J. E. Lewin, Trans.). Ithaca, NY: Cornell University Press.

Golden, J. M. (1986). Story interpretation as a group process. *English Quarterly, 19,* 254–266.

Golden, J. M. (1990). *The narrative symbol in childhood literature: Explorations in the construction of text.* Berlin, New York: de Gruyter.

Golden, J. M., & Canan, D. (1998, July). *Students' questions and the construction of a literary work.* Paper presented at the World Congress on Reading, Ochos Rios, Jamaica.

Golden, J. M., & Gerber, A. (1990). A semiotic perspective of text: The picture story book event. *Journal of Reading Behavior: A Journal of Literacy, 22,* 203–219.

Golden, J. M., & Gerber, A. (1992). The sign of a tale: The literary symbol in a classroom context. *Semiotica, 89*(1/3), 35–46.

Golden, J. M., & Guthrie, J. T. (1986). Convergence and divergence in reader response to literature. *Reading Research Quarterly, 21*(4), 408–421.

Golden, J. M., & Handloff, E. (1993). Responding to literature through journal writing. In K. Holland, R. Hungerford, & S. Ernst (Eds.), *Journeying: Children responding to literature* (pp. 175–186). Portsmouth, NH: Heinemann.

Golden, J. M., & Zuniga-Hill, C. (1990, April). *Parent–sibling interactions with a three-year-old during book reading events*. Paper presented at the American Educational Research Convention, Boston, MA.

Goodman, K. S. (1987). Look what they've done to Judy Blume!: The "basalization" of children's literature. *The New Advocate, 1*(1), 29–41.

Green, J., & Harker, J. (1987). *Multiple perspective analysis*. Norwood, NJ: Ablex.

Green, J. L., & Golden, J. M. (1983). *Storytelling project*. Unpublished curriculum project, University of Delaware, Newark.

Green, J. L., & Smith, D. (1983). Teaching and learning: A linguistic perspective. *The Elementary School Journal, 83*, 353–391.

Green, J. L., & Wallat, C. (1981). *Ethnography and language in educational settings*. Norwood, NJ: Ablex.

Green, J. L., Weade, G., & Graham, K. (1988). Lesson construction and student participation: A sociolinguistic analysis. In J. L. Green & J. O. Harker (Eds.), *Multiple perspective analyses of classroom discourse* (pp. 11–47). Norwood, NJ: Ablex.

Grimm, J., & Grimm, W. , illustrated by Bernadette.(1971). *Little Red Riding Hood*. New York: Scholastic Book Services.

Gumperz, J. (1986). Interactional sociolinguistics in the study of schooling. In J. Cook-Gumperz (Ed.), *The social construction of literacy* (pp. 45–68). Cambridge, UK: Cambridge University Press.

Guy, R. (1979). *The friends*. New York: Bantam.

Halliday, M. A. K. (1978). *Language as social semiotic: The social interpretation of language and meaning*. Baltimore, MD: University Park Press.

Hamilton, V. (1983). *Sweet whispers, brother rush*. New York: Philomel.

Heath, S. B. (1983). *Ways with words*. Cambridge, UK: Cambridge University Press.

Henry, M. (1948). *King of the wind*. New York: Scholastic.

Hiebert, E. (1991). Teacher-based assessment of literacy learning. In I. J. Flood, J. Jensen, D. Lapp, & J. Squire (Eds.), *Handbook of research on the teaching of language arts* (pp. 510–520). New York: MacMillan.

Hobbs, W. (1989). *Bearstone*. New York: Atheneum.

Hodge, R. (1990). *Literature as discourse: Textual strategies in English and history*. Cambridge, UK: Polity Press.

Hodge, R., & Kress, G. (1988). *Social semiotics*. Ithaca, NY: Cornell University Press.

Huck, C., Heplar, S., Hickman, J., & Kiefer, B. (1997). *Children's literature in the elementary school* (6th ed.). Madison, WI: Brown & Benchmark.

Hutchins, P. (1968). *Rosie's walk*. New York: MacMillan.

Hymes, D. (1974). *Foundation in sociolinguistics*. Philadelphia: University of Pennsylvania Press.

Iser, W. (1978). *The act of reading: A theory of aesthetic response*. Baltimore: The Johns Hopkins University Press.

Jackson, P. (1968). *Life in classrooms*. New York: Holt, Rinehart & Winston.

Keats, E. J. (1962). *The snowy day*. New York: Viking.

Keats, E. J. (1969). *Goggles*. New York: MacMillan.

Keats, E. J. (1970). *Hi Cat!* New York: MacMillan.

Kellog, S. (1977). *The mysterious tadpole*. New York: Dial.

King, M., & Rentel, V. (1981). *How children learn to write: A longitudinal study* (Final report to the National Institute of Education). Washington, DC: National Institute of Education.

Kjelgaard, J. (1975). Blood on the Ice. In G. R. Carlsen (Ed.) *Perception: Themes in literature* (pp. 249–254). New York: McGraw-Hill.

Lemke, J. L. (1990). *Talking science: Language, learning, and values*. Norwood, NJ: Ablex.

Lemke, J. L. (1995). *Textual politics: Discourse and social dynamics*. London, UK: Taylor & Francis.

Lessing, D. (1975). A mild attack of locusts. In G. R. Carlsen (Ed.), *Perception: Themes in literature* (pp. 355–360). New York: McGraw-Hill.

Liebling, C. (1989). Inside view and character plans in an original story and its basal adaptation. *Theory Into Practice, 28*(2), 88–97.

Lionni, L. (1964). *Swimmy*. New York: Pantheon.

Lionni, L. (1989). Swimmy. In *Upon a shore* (pp. 142–149). New York: MacMillan/McGraw Hill School Publishing.

Mandler, J., & Johnson, N. (1977). Remembrance of things parsed: Story understanding and recall. *Cognitive Psychology, 11*, 111–151.

Mayer, M. (1973). *What do you do with a kangaroo?* New York: Ashton Scholastic.

McDermott, R. (1978). Relating and learning. An analysis of two classroom reading groups. In R. Shuy (Ed.), *Linguistics and reading*. Rowley, MA: Newbury House.

Mehan, H. (1979). *Learning lessons: Social organization in the classroom*. Cambridge, MA: Harvard University Press.

Michaels, S. (1981). Sharing time: Children's narrative styles and differential access to literacy. *Language in Society, 10*, 423–442.

Moore, J. N. (1997). *Interpreting young adult literature: Literary theory in the secondary classroom*. Portsmouth, NH: Boynton/Cook.

Myers, W. D. (1988). *Scorpions*. New York: Harper Trophy.

Nodelman, P. (1988). *Words about pictures: The narrative art of children's picture books*. Athens: The University of Georgia Press.

Ortony, A. (1985). Theoretical and methodological issues in the study of metaphor. In C. Cooper (Ed.), *Researching response to literature and the teaching of literature: Points of departure* (pp. 151–168). Norwood, NJ: Ablex.

Paterson, K. (1978). *Bridge to Terebithia*. New York: Crowell.

Peirce, C. S. (1932). *Collected papers of Charles Sanders Peirce* (Vol. II; C. Hartshorne & P. Weiss, Eds.). Cambridge, MA: Harvard University Press.

Perrault, C. (1974). The little red riding hood. In I. Opie & P. Opie (Eds.), *The classic fairy tales*. New York: Oxford University Press.

Polanyi, M. (1966). *The tacit dimension*. Garden City, NY: Doubleday.

Raskins, E. (1966). *Nothing ever happens on my block*. New York: Scholastic Books.

Rimmon-Kenan, S. (1983). *Narrative fiction: Contemporary poetics*. London, New York: Methuen.

Rosenblatt, L. (1976). *Literature as exploration*. New York: Noble & Noble.

Scholes, R. (1985). *Textual power*. New Haven, CT: Yale University Press.

Scholes, R. (1982). *Semiotics and interpretation*. New Haven, CT: Yale University Press.

Sendak, M. (1963). *Where the wild things are*. New York: Harper.

Snow, C. E., & Ninio, A. (1986). The contracts of literacy: What children learn from learning to read books. In W. H. Teale & E. Sulzby (Eds.), *Emergent literacy: writing and reading*. Norwood, NJ: Ablex.

Spinelli, J. (1990). *Maniac McGee*. New York: HarperCollins.

Thibault, P. (1991). *Social semiotics as praxis: Text, social meaning making, and Nabakov's Ada*. Minneapolis, MN: University of Minnesota Press.

van Allsburg, C. (1990). *Just a dream*. Boston: Houghton Mifflin.

van Dijk, T. A., & Kintsch, W. (1983). *Strategies of discourse comprehension*. New York: Academic Press.

West, J. (1943). Reverdy. *New Mexico Quarterly Review, 13*, 21–27.

Wilder, L. I. (1953). *Little house in the big woods*. New York: Harper & Row.

Zemach, H. (1965). *Salt: A Russian tale*. New York: Follett.

Zindel, P. (1968). *The pigman*. New York: Harper & Row.

Zipes, J. (1983). *Fairy tales and the art of subversion*. New York: Methuen.

# Author Index

# Subject Index

## A

Access to texts, 129, 147
Altering texts, for instructional purposes, 33–37, 130
    types of alterations, 33
Articulated text, 100
Assessment(s) of students, 7–8, 18, 101
    using a range of methods, 148
Attentiveness of students, 121–122

## B

Biographies, 138, 139
    "authentic" vs. fictionalized, 138–139
*Blood on the Ice* (Kjelgaard), 24–25

## C

Channels
    of learning, range of, 145, *see also* Picture storybooks
    text, 6, 18
Character(s)
    feelings of, 109–110
    "reading"/construction of, 20–21, 89, 123, 142–143
    taking on the role of, 58–59
Classrooms
    as unique meaning-making enterprises, 7
    as unique semiotic systems, 4–8
    as variant semiotic systems, 8–9
Classroom (text) events, 16–17, *see also* specific topics

expectations regarding, 103, 115–116, 146
    reasons for studying, 9–10
Communicative competence, 132
    indications of, 132–136
Communicative task framework, 16–17
Community, 134
Complexity of literature, range in, 145–146
Constructing stories, 83–84, 132–134, *see also* Reactive texts
    in different contexts, 134–135
Context(s), 44, 48
    constructing stories in different, 134–135
    social, 15–17
    texts embedded in, 149–150
Contextual demands for meaning-making, 17
Contextualizing narratives, 84–85
Cues, textual, 19, 20, 37–38, 43, 79
    in novels, 20–25
    in picture storybooks, 26–32, 59, *see also* Picture story book events
"Cultural" units, grouping texts into, 144
Cultural values transmitted by teachers, 16, *see also* Multiculturalism
Current events narratives, 137–138

## D

Disagreements between students, 62–63
Discourse, 7, 13–15, 44
    defined, 15
    kinds of, 18